The Essential Guide to
Anorexia

ROBERT D ITOR

Published in Great Britain in 2018 by

need2know

Remus House

Coltsfoot Drive

Peterborough

PE2 9BF

Telephone 01733 898103

www.need2knowbooks.co.uk

SB ISBN 978-1-91084-397-0

Cover photograph: Adobe Stock

Contents

Chapter 6: Letting Go – Stepping Towards Recovery 59

Chapter 7: Staying Safe – Preventing Relapse 73

Chapter 8: Keeping Up the Fight: The Onward Journey 81

Help List 87

Introduction

I am not a doctor, nor am I a dietician or a therapist. I have no qualifications in healthcare or psychology. I do not even work in the mental health sector. What I do have is years of personal experience, suffering with and recovering from anorexia and bulimia, and I believe this has given me an insight into and understanding of eating disorders that other authors and experts simply do not have. I do not know all there is to know and I certainly do not have the cure, but I do know that I can help you come to a deeper and more realistic understanding of anorexia; whether you are anorexic or not.

Anorexia is a serious mental illness which is too often stereotyped, glamorised, misunderstood, simplified and belittled. It is natural to want to have someone or something to blame when we find ourselves faced with a seemingly unfair situation that makes no sense to us. We ask questions and we want to point the finger; we strive to come to some kind of clear-cut conclusion, an explanation of what has gone wrong and why. This is where we run into problems.

There can be no simple, straightforward explanation for an illness as extremely complex as anorexia nervosa. Eating disorders affect around 1.6 million people in the UK, and although anorexia isn't the most common, it is the most deadly. Characterised by an overwhelming fear of weight gain, those affected dramatically reduce their food intake and may also overexercise, vomit or use laxatives in a desperate bid to lose weight.

Anorexia does not discriminate. It affects people of all ages, genders, ethnicity, race and religion. Anorexia is often thought of as something that is exclusive to young, white, middle and upper class females; a vain attempt to fit in with the idealistic image of a 'perfect body' portrayed by the media and fashion industries as something we should all aspire to be. None of this is true and I hope that this book will allow me to explain why. I hope to expel the myths and stereotypes that exist about anorexia and help you to understand the true meaning of anorexia – above and beyond those age-old explanations that only ever scratch the surface.

1

Setting it Straight – What is Anorexia?

The definition of anorexia

A norexia is a mental illness which affects an estimated 1.6 million people in the UK. It is characterised by an intense fear of weight gain which causes people with the illness to go to extreme lengths to restrict what they eat in order to lose weight. People with anorexia also tend to see themselves as fat or overweight even when they are very underweight, making it very difficult for them to recognise the problem.

It is something that is commonly discussed and debated amongst doctors, teachers, medical professionals, journalists and almost everyone else. We see pictures, hear stories and read articles on anorexia all the time, so it is really important that we truly understand what it is, what it means and what impact it has on all those affected by it.

Origins

The definition of anorexia nervosa differs depending on where you look. If we break it down into the Greek prefix an- (negation of) and orexis (appetite), it literally means a lack of desire to eat. Add in 'nervosa' and it changes to a neurotic loss of appetite. Unfortunately, this definition can be misleading and that is probably one of the reasons there has been, and still is, so much confusion around the illness.

The reality

Anorexia is much more than a simple lack of appetite. It is laced with complexities which defy logic and justification. Many have tried to accurately define anorexia, but there have always been exceptions to the rules, with National Institute for Health and Clinical Excellence (NICE) guidelines having to be reconsidered and rewritten in order to encompass those exceptions.

In my own words, anorexia nervosa is a destructive mental illness characterised by a fear of gaining weight, forcing sufferers to go to extreme lengths to ensure this cannot and will not happen, often leading to an obsession which takes over that person's whole life.

Ask anybody who has experienced anorexia what it means to them and they will each have their own definition to give; no two stories will be the same. Each person will have their own triggers, their own behaviours, rituals, thoughts and feelings; hence the fact that we cannot ever pin it down to one simple explanation.

One thing we must learn, understand and remember is that anorexia is a mental illness, a mental illness which destroys lives and even kills; but also one that can be treated, fought and beaten.

Other eating disorders can be overlooked, so although this book is about anorexia, another thing we need to be aware of is that anorexia is not the only eating disorder, and despite what most people might think, it isn't even the most common.

'One thing we must learn, understand and remember is that anorexia is a mental illness, a mental illness which destroys lives and even kills; but also one that can be treated, fought and beaten.'

Some facts and figures

- An estimated 1.6 million people in the UK are directly affected by an eating disorder.
- 10% of those have anorexia.
- 40% have bulimia.

- The remaining 50% fall into the EDNOS (Eating Disorder Not Otherwise Specified) category, which includes BED (Binge-eating Disorder), COE (Compulsive Overeating) and a mixture of both bulimia and anorexia.

- Without treatment, up to 20% of people with anorexia will die as a result.

- Around 46% of people with anorexia make a full recovery.

Again, as with the definitions, these statistics are not completely accurate. I will go into more detail about why later in the book, but when looking at the number of people who suffer with anorexia, it is important to remember that there are many who keep their condition completely under wraps, do not seek treatment or do not have access to treatment, and are therefore not included in the statistics. This makes it very difficult to make such estimations or rely on figures. If anything, though, this 1.6 million figure is likely to be an underestimation of the true total and that alone tells us that this is a huge problem which affects too many people.

Anorexia needs to be taken seriously, treated with respect and given the time it deserves to be truly understood. The more we educate and spread awareness about anorexia, the less stigma there will be and together we can create a society where sufferers feel that they can speak out and ask for help without feeling scared or ashamed.

Common myths and stereotypes

Anorexia is extremely complex and therefore, very easily misunderstood. As it is so often discussed and reported across the media, many people presume they know everything there is to know about the illness, but many of these articles and comments are misinformed and contain misconceptions, myths and stereotypes that are passed on as truth. I will address the issue of the media in chapter 3, but there are many common myths and stereotypes that should be explained here. In order to paint a clear picture and form an educated understanding of what anorexia is, it is vital to learn what it is not.

Anorexia is not:

- About vanity. It is a mental illness, much more concerned with how people feel rather than look.

- An illness that only affects young women. It can happen to absolutely anyone.

- A lifestyle choice. Nobody chooses to suffer from anorexia.

- Just a phase. Anorexia can last for years and even after recovery, it can have a permanent impact both physically and mentally.

- Always visible. Not all people with anorexia will become as emaciated as many media reports would have us believe, they may appear a healthy weight.

- A dislike of food. In fact, many people with anorexia never stop thinking about food.

- All about weight. Anorexia is characterised by constant mental torture, anguish and obsessive behaviours.

- Glamorous, in any way whatsoever.

- Always to do with control. There are many different reasons why people develop anorexia.

- Easily treatable. Recovery is a very long, arduous and complex journey. Anorexia is not fixed with a simple meal plan or self-help guide.

- The end. There is always hope, no matter how severe the case of anorexia is. Recovery is possible, and it is worth the hard work and heartache.

'Nobody decides that they will be anorexic, nor do they choose to continue down that destructive path.'

The reality of anorexia and the devastating impact that it has on all those directly affected is quite often far detached from the impression we are given by magazines, television programmes and even some newspapers. The problem with this is that people tend to believe what they see and read, so if the facts are not right in the first place, anything that is said is passed on as fact. The cycle continues, we are constantly fed these inaccurate descriptions and explanations, and myths and stereotypes are continually perpetuated.

As a result of these misconceptions, some people form very narrow-minded opinions and perceptions of people with anorexia. Some come to believe that anorexia is not an illness, but something that young girls and women choose to do in a desperate attempt to look like size 0 models. The 'pro-ana' movement certainly has not helped dissipate this view, as some of those websites offer dangerous tips on how to become anorexic, but that does not make it true. Nobody decides that they will be anorexic, nor do they choose to continue down that destructive path.

Another common belief that forms as a result of the list of myths and stereotypes mentioned previously is that once a person with anorexia has gone through treatment, they are then well, fully recovered. Again, this is not true. Seeking help and getting treatment is the first and most important step, but what recovery does is introduce an anorexic to a set of tools; therapies and techniques which are designed to help them cope with their eating disorder and the emotions that come with that. Even when someone who has anorexia has gained weight and appears to be in full health, it is highly likely that they are still struggling with anorexic thoughts such as guilt, low self-esteem and a distorted perception of their own appearance.

The physical effects

The physical effects of anorexia are many and varied. Some people with anorexia will display all of the following, whilst others may only experience a few. Problems such as heart problems, tooth decay and osteoporosis will develop over a long period of time and some of these can have a lasting impact on the body. However, if anorexia is successfully treated then damage limitation is possible to an extent. Obviously, the sooner these effects and the whole illness is treated, the better the outcome.

Remember, each individual is different. This is just a list of possible effects, not a diagnostic criteria:

- Severe weight loss
- Amenorrhoea (periods stopping)
- Insomnia
- Abdominal pains
- Constipation and bloating
- Poor circulation and feeling cold
- Aching, tired limbs
- Lack of energy and weakness
- Dry skin
- Brittle nails
- Thinning hair
- Dizziness, headaches and fainting
- Tooth decay and gum damage
- Bruising
- Lanugo – fine layer of hair all over the body

- Low blood pressure, slow heart rate, palpitations and even heart failure
- Anaemia and other blood problems
- Osteoporosis

In addition to restricted eating, people with anorexia may also develop other behaviours to rid themselves of calories, burn calories or lose weight in other ways. One method is by making themselves sick after eating or abusing laxatives, sometimes called anorexia nervosa purging subtype. This brings with it another set of risks and dangers to the body, listed below.

Physical effects of self-induced vomiting and/or laxative abuse:

- Fluctuating weight
- Headaches
- Sore throat
- Scarred knuckles
- Dehydration causing electrolyte imbalances
- Oesophageal tears causing bleeding
- Dizziness
- Stomach ulcers or other complications
- Irregular heartbeat and other cardiac problems which could result in heart failure or death.

These risks emphasise just how dangerous and serious an illness anorexia is. But when somebody with anorexia is aware of all of the risks and even when they have suffered physically as a result of their restrictive eating, the illness still drives them to continue. Quite often, an anorexic will know exactly what danger their body is in, but the fear of gaining weight is too intense to allow them to want to change.

'Quite often, an anorexic will know exactly what danger their body is in, but the fear of gaining weight is too intense to allow them to want to change.'

The psychological effects

This brings us on to the psychological aspect of the illness, the effects that anorexia has on the mind, thought processes and behaviours. Starving the body of the nutrients it needs to function does not only have a physical impact, it has a direct and powerful effect on the brain. Here is a list of some of the possible psychological effects of anorexia:

- Intense fear of gaining weight

- Depression

- Mood swings

- Irritability

- Lack of concentration

- Distorted body image

- Obsessive thoughts about food and weight

- Feelings of guilt and shame after eating

- Desire to withdraw, to become isolated

- Compulsions to exercise, purge or fast

- Feelings of worthlessness

A bit of background – My story

At the tender age of 7, I scribbled in a school exercise book that my New Year's resolution was to lose weight. I don't remember writing this and I don't remember thinking that I needed to lose weight, but that thought must have been somewhere ingrained in my mind from that age, and there it remained.

I began to throw away my dinner every lunchtime. I remember that, because I had to become increasingly cunning in my bid to go unnoticed. That deceptive child who denied all knowledge of anything being wrong whenever asked grew into a teenager who would go most of the day fuelled by diet drinks and snap at anyone who asked if she was eating properly. I didn't stop eating completely; anorexic people rarely do, but I was very underweight for my height and it became obvious to friends, teachers and family that something wasn't right.

The first, reluctant trip to the doctors was a disaster for my parents and a triumph for me. Their concerns were dismissed and they were told it was 'probably just a phase'. To me, the fact that a doctor had said that made me feel that it was fine to carry on doing what I was doing, to continue my path of destruction.

During sixth form, my weight decreased slowly as I skipped more meals, exercised more often and sank deeper into a dark world of depression, self-harm and routine starvation. Still, although there was concern and worry all around me, I batted off any comments, and those closest to me were afraid to bring up my dwindling weight, knowing that I would shut it out, lock myself away and refuse to talk or admit it was a problem. I must have been very difficult indeed.

Things escalated and became unmanageable during my first year of university. For me, moving away from home and living with people who did not know me spelt out freedom; it flung open the doors for me to do whatever I wanted, whenever I wanted and nobody was there to stop me or tell me how to live. I didn't have to pretend that I was OK and there was nobody around who felt it was their duty to look after me. By this point, I was incapable of looking after myself and as a consequence, the little I was living on decreased even further and so did my mood.

At the time, I thought I was happy, I thought that as the number on the scale went down, I was congratulating myself because I was doing something right and showing that I had the determination to restrain myself and resist the temptations that everybody else succumbed to so easily. I was pleased with my progress and proud of the fact that I could go for days without anything solid entering my digestive system. It made me feel powerful, indestructible and invincible. I couldn't have been further from the truth. In reality, I was miserable, lonely, withdrawn, isolated, desperately ill, fighting to function, constantly tired and cold to the bone; at a time when I felt I had control over everything, I had actually lost all control. I needed help, I just wouldn't admit it.

It was only when I was threatened with being sectioned under the Mental Health Act that I finally realised, or truly acknowledged the seriousness of my illness. I started seeing a counsellor back home but in Aberystwyth, where I was studying, there was no help apart from my GP and so, despite gaining enough weight to keep me out of hospital, my behaviours worsened. I exercised more, started binging and purging, using laxatives, and even ordered pills from the Internet. I knew how dangerous all these drastic actions were, but all I cared about was my constant fear of gaining weight.

Somehow, I managed to complete university and build an amazing circle of friends who accepted me for who I was, not what I was. I came away with a first degree in Film and Television Studies, but even that achievement paled in comparison to losing weight.

It was then that I decided enough was enough, I was sick and tired of being sick and tired and I knew that if I wanted to build a better future for myself, things had to change. I knew that I was unable to get better without proper help, so for the first time ever, I was completely honest with my doctor and therapist and was referred for inpatient treatment at a specialist eating disorder unit.

Recovery is a long journey. For me, it has taken years to get to a healthy weight, cut out anorexic and bulimic behaviours and most importantly, accept my body as it is, treat it well and appreciate what it can do when I take proper care of it. This process is not easy; it has taken two hospitalisations and enough blood, sweat and tears to fill many swimming pools to get me this far.

What I can say though, is that recovery is possible and it is worth it.

'Recovery is possible and it is worth it.'

Summing Up

- Anorexia is a very complex, serious mental illness.

- Anorexia can have a severe impact on the health of the body and mind.

- Anorexia can kill but full recovery is possible.

- Anorexia is one of many eating disorders and it is not the most common.

- Anorexia has two main subtypes: restrictive and purging.

- Anorexia can happen to anyone at any time.

- Anorexia is often misunderstood due to common myths and stereotypes.

- Everyone has their own experience and their own story, no two cases are the same.

- The more we understand about anorexia, the better for everyone.

2

The Illness That Doesn't Discriminate

Who gets anorexia?

Going back to the common myths and stereotypes about anorexia, perhaps the most common misconception is that anorexia is an illness which only affects young, white, middle-to-upper-class females. They are all high-achieving perfectionists who are influenced by the bombardment of images of 'the perfect body', size 0 models and bone-thin celebrities who are splashed across glossy magazines.

This could not be further from the truth. Anorexia does not discriminate, it can affect anybody at any stage in their life regardless of age, gender, race, religion or sexual orientation. As with any other mental illness, nobody chooses to become anorexic and any number of events or conditions can be a trigger.

It has been reported in recent years that there have been huge increases in the numbers of males, children and older people suffering with anorexia and other eating disorders. However, it is difficult to tell whether the number is really growing, or whether it is due to the fact that more people feel able to speak out about it as a result of spreading awareness and breaking down stigma. If it is the former, we need to make sure that we are open to understanding that these groups can suffer from anorexia and help create a society in which they feel able to reach out for help. If it is the latter, we need to continue building on this and ensure that everyone who has anorexia has access to suitable treatment without fear of discrimination of any kind.

Anorexia in males

It is almost impossible to estimate the number of males who have anorexia. The statistics are varying and conflicting, with most only reflecting the number of men who are actually admitted to hospital for treatment, quite a small minority of all sufferers. It is estimated that 11% of the 1.6 million people in the UK who have eating disorders are male and reports from the Royal College of Practitioners indicated a 66% rise of male hospital admissions. The statistics are quite staggering, but as there is still so much stigma attached to male eating disorders, hence many suffering in silence, this could be the tip of the iceberg.

'Anorexia is most likely to develop in males between the ages of 14 and 25.'

Age of onset

Anorexia is most likely to develop in males between the ages of 14 and 25, but again, it can affect people at any age, onset can start at any time in someone's life for any number of reasons.

Stigma

There has been an increase in awareness and coverage of male eating disorders in the media in recent years, especially thanks to charities set up specifically with this in mind.

MGEDT (Men Get Eating Disorders Too) is a prime example of this. Set up in 2008 by Sam Thomas, who suffered from an eating disorder throughout his teen and early adult years, MGEDT is an award-winning charity which educates and informs a huge audience across the UK. After his own experience, Sam realised that there was very little, if any, information about eating disorders available specifically for males, so he took it upon himself to set up a website to help those who found themselves in the same position – looking for help but not knowing where to find it.

The charity aims not only to provide information, educating people about the very specific needs of men with eating disorders, but also to enable men who have eating disorders to connect with others in similar situations, encouraging them to break down the walls of secretiveness and isolation which characterise the illness, especially when combined with the stigma attached to male eating disorders.

To find out more visit the MGEDT website www.mengetedstoo.co.uk, and see the help list for further contact details.

The stigma I refer to is slowly being broken down, but there are still deeply ingrained stereotypes and ill-informed perceptions ofwho gets an eating disorder. There is still that belief that anorexia is a girls' illness, so amongst men, that only adds to the feelings of shame that people with eating disorders tend to experience regardless of gender.

We always tend to obsess over the fact that women are expected to look a certain way, aspire towards certain body shapes and attempt to copy unrealistic ideals portrayed to us through glossy magazines. We are told that women have to be thin to be successful, that we should emulate those we idolise by analysing their dietary habits, copying them, counting points and squealing in delight as the number on the scales goes down. But we forget about men.

In the same way that women's magazines are too often lacking in normal, average-sized women, not airbrushed and untouched, so are men's. Male models who used to be so well built, masculine, buff even, are now fitting into the same skinny jeans as their female counterparts. The expectations placed on men now are so mixed that there is no wonder there is confusion and fear when it comes to how they should feel about their own bodies, never mind how difficult it must be for them to voice any concerns. Men are supposed to be strong but anorexia is seen as a huge weakness. Nobody wants to admit that, least of all males.

> 'Men are supposed to be strong but anorexia is seen as a huge weakness. Nobody wants to admit that, least of all males.'

Liam's story

'It's a phase', 'A growth spurt', and the best one, 'Just go home and eat a bowl of porridge and a slice of pizza'. These were just some of the quotes of several medical professionals in the lead up to my diagnosis of anorexia.

As I male, I feel that an eating disorder would have been the last thing I would have, as boys and young men aspire to look 'buff', 'muscular', 'macho'. I was the opposite, all I wanted was to be thin. In my head 'thin' was fit and healthy. It would mean that I would appear confident, respected and successful… How wrong I was.

As a child and at the beginning of my teenage years I had a large amount of 'puppy fat'. When I was 11, my dad left and so, my home life changed dramatically. I found all of my comfort in food, my relationship was with food. I'd cook for the family and kept myself happy with treats of McDonald's, pizza and chocolate.

By the age of 13, I knew that I wanted to have a singing career, I was set on it. At school though, I was bullied due to my size, my high voice and my soon-to-be discovered sexuality. As a response, I took drastic action; I decreased my food intake and hid it well and for many years. Long before I was officially diagnosed with anorexia nervosa at 19, it was apparent that I was ill. But as so many do, I hid it away from the outside world.

The first time I realised I had a eating problem was when I started university. My tutors got involved after my first boyfriend went to them. My parents soon noticed too; the change in my personality and the drastic and horrifying weight loss when I returned back home finally gave my secret away.

Still, despite my acknowledgement and their growing worries, I continued to decrease my intake and upped my exercise. Then one day I just collapsed. I was rushed to hospital in cardiac arrest; my heart in overdrive, and organ failure. Threatened with being sectioned under the Mental Health Act, I agreed to being admitted for specialist treatment.

It was those long, hard 6 months I spent in the eating disorder clinic that really got me back on my feet. It was a huge struggle, but in time, I did make progress. My family really supported me and after discharge, helped at home, with travels to daycare, therapy sessions and check-ups.

Other than allowing myself to come to terms with having a life-changing mental illness, the one thing I found the most upsetting was seeing the impact I was having on those around me. My family were heartbroken, they blamed themselves because no matter what they said or did, they couldn't change my thought processes or actions. My friends were very confused and sadly, I did lose some as anorexia changed me completely. I became a nasty person, totally consumed in my eating habits and exercise regimes.

But now I have friends who have stuck by me and finally disconnected themselves with how I was and how I looked.

As for the medical profession, I helped open their eyes a little. A far cry from my first extremely unhelpful experiences, my local surgery now have a fantastic doctor who has been there through all the ups and downs and did extensive research into eating disorders, different therapies and had a lot of contact with the unit where I was treated. I think eating disorders are becoming more equal in males and females. Not that this is a good thing, but at least the awareness of this increase in males with anorexia and bulimia makes it easier to speak out, and hopefully sufferers will be treated before things get out of hand or they are misdiagnosed.

Not long after leaving hospital, Liam was accepted into a school of dance and drama in New York and is now following his dream of having a career in singing.

Anorexia in children

The reported number of children being treated for anorexia has been rising for a number of years and fears are growing that this trend will continue. Children as young as 6 are receiving inpatient treatment for anorexia and the majority of all cases admitted to hospital are between the ages of 14 and 19.

Again, we should not rely on statistics to tell us the true story of exactly what is happening; it is much easier to slip through the net and go on living and functioning as an anorexic when your are an adult. If a child is ill, in most cases, their parents or guardians will do everything they can to make sure they get the right treatment, so one would presume that most children who do show signs of having anorexia will be referred to a specialist. Of course, this is not always the case.

Why do children become anorexic?

There are constant reports about obesity in children, which does affect far more young people than anorexia. Not a day goes by that there is no mention of obesity, junk food and health problems caused by poor, unbalanced diets; and increasingly, this is geared not only towards the parents responsible, but at the children themselves.

With so much constant, intense bombardment of warnings, scares and shocking statistics, it is easy to see why young people are growing up with an increased knowledge, accurate or not, about a certain idea of what it is to be healthy. Most worryingly of all is that so many children now are being taught to differentiate between 'good' and 'bad' foods, a kind of black and white thinking that goes completely against the idea of establishing a healthy, balanced diet. This black and white approach is dangerous. At such a young age, strong connections are made and behaviours and thought patterns are developed. To be told that something which should be seen as a treat, for example chocolate, is 'bad' should be seen as planting a seed, which may be

'Children as young as 6 are receiving inpatient treatment for anorexia and the majority of all cases admitted to hospital are between the ages of 14 and 19.'

ignored as that child grows, but could potentially be the start of something a lot more serious. If that child wants to be 'good' and healthy, there is a strong chance they will follow every bit of advice they are given about how they should act, and if avoiding 'bad' foods is what they are told to do, that is what they will do. It sounds very simplistic, but children are so attentive to messages we send out to them, that they will pick up on negative connotations and develop unhealthy attitudes to food and weight.

Dictated diets – good and bad

We all know that a young child's diet depends almost exclusively on what their parents or guardians eat; whether they eat all meals together at certain times round the table or they help themselves, home-cooked food or ready-meals and takeaways, occasional special treats or cupboards packed with sweets and crisps to which they help themselves. Often, it is the early years that count and that give a grounding in, quite simply, how to eat; with a routine or without, consciously or not. Without oversimplifying, anyone can look at a family and more or less determine whether the children are growing up in a healthy or an unhealthy environment. Either extreme could be damaging without taking into account any external factors or messages picked up as the children develop. Too strict and a child may develop fears of certain foods, or be tempted to overindulge on the things that are restricted at home when they are old enough to do so. Too lax and children will develop no sense of set mealtimes, routine, control or discipline.

Children form very strong, powerful and definite ideas and beliefs about food and weight from an extremely young age and now, as we are constantly told that we are feeding our kids too much rubbish and hammering home this message that fruit and vegetables are good and pizza and crisps are bad, those initial thoughts are being confirmed at an ever-increasing intensity. The relationship between children and food/weight would ideally be balanced, but that, worryingly, is becoming a rarity.

Considering all the conflicting messages, ill-informed ideals and incessant scare stories, there is no wonder why we have an obesity crisis. The problem is that we are only just realising that there is an impact on the other end of the scale too, not only do we have a growing number of obese children, we also have more and more anorexic children and teenagers.

Lack of awareness

The most frustrating thing about this situation is that many cases are likely to be preventable and the reason rates have been increasing year on year has to be down to a lack of awareness and understanding. There have been too many cases of parents taking their children to their doctor, explaining the symptoms, telling them that they are not eating and losing weight, and they are being told to come back in six months time. Again, the earlier anorexia is caught, the better.

Anorexia, like obesity, can be picked up and prevented before it gets to the stage where intensive, expert help is needed. Not only would opening our eyes to this save money, it would also save lives.

The same stereotypical response exists for child anorexia as it does in adult anorexia. The media and fashion worlds are again blamed for portraying unrealistic ideals and skinny role models who children look up to and aspire to look like. The media blame pop stars, celebrities and clothing chains who use unhealthy looking models, under the presumption that all children who have anorexia are sucked into believing that they too have to be thin and pretty. It is just not that simple.

We are too scared to point the finger at the people in real life, who see these children every day; the parents who worry but don't know where to turn, the teachers who notice children skipping lunches but cast a blind eye, the teaching assistants who overhear children discussing calories and weight and competing against each other and the GPs who 'wait and see'. There are so many people at so many different points who, if they knew the signs and took them as seriously as they ought to, could make a massive difference to the overall outcome.

We cannot prevent eating disorders, no one can and no one ever will, but we can prevent them from worsening, we can detect them at the early stages and treat them before these children become so entrenched in the illness that their lives will be dictated by it and punctuated with long stays in treatment centres.

'Anorexia, like obesity, can be picked up and prevented before it gets to the stage where intensive, expert help is needed.'

Ignorance is not the solution

Anorexia makes people devious and sneaky, no matter what their age. We hide it well and we lie to our parents about what food we have or haven't eaten. I know for a fact that as I was growing up, many people picked up on my habits, comments and weight loss, and I hope that now, things have changed. I hope that anybody who does notice these things knows how important it is to speak up about it, raise concerns and keep doing so until they get a response. We wait too much now. Dinner ladies, sports coaches, swimming teachers, school teachers, school nurses, head teachers, deputies, tell the parents or guardians. Parents or guardians, when you approach a child who you suspect might have an eating problem, he/she will most likely pretend that nothing is wrong, but if you are worried, don't let this put you off. Don't ignore the problem, don't push it aside, get to the doctor and be open and honest; push for answers and if necessary, specialist help.

Anorexia in older people

'Anorexia is increasingly affecting older women and men, with the reported numbers rising steadily over the last 5 years.'

Although the majority of recorded cases of admissions for anorexia are for those under the age of 20, there are many more people suffering who are older, sometimes much older, and this often goes undetected. The recent statistics enforce the stereotype that anorexia is a teenage girls' illness, but it is really important that we understand that what we see in the news is often just the tip of the iceberg in terms of how many people really suffer from eating disorders.

Again, the statistics only tell half of the story, but from personal experience, I have known many older people who have been affected by anorexia for many years but have continued to live and function as well as they possibly could for as long as they could before getting the treatment they needed. I met one woman who was 68 and was receiving treatment for the first time after many years of illness, so her story proved to me that there must be many more older people out there who have anorexia, but are not counted amongst the others whenever new reports are published.

How and why does anorexia affect the older generation?

Anorexia is increasingly affecting older women and men, with the reported numbers rising steadily over the last 5 years. This could be partly due to the increase in awareness of the fact that anorexia can affect people of all ages, but experts believe that the rise is actually the result of more younger people slipping through the net and growing old with anorexia as part (or all) of their lives. That is in addition to an increase in those developing the illness at a later age, for any number of reasons.

Media misperceptions

One of these reasons could be that there is an undeniable and increasing pressure on women and men to look younger for longer. We are constantly bombarded with advertising aimed at anti-ageing and are surrounded by images of celebrities who appear to defy the ageing process. What slips our minds when we see such images though, is that the likes of Madonna, Michelle Pfeiffer and Brad Pitt employ full-time personal trainers, stylists and make-up artists, and many of the older celebrities we see looking 10 or 20 years younger have had a little help in the form of plastic surgery and/or airbrushing. These 'role models' are not realistic portrayals of what us 'normal' people will look like as we get older, but they are certainly hard to avoid and therefore, we are putting more effort than ever into countering the effects of getting old.

As with younger people with anorexia, this notion that it is caused by the images we see of celebrities and models is only a very small part of the problem. A person has to show other signs of vulnerability, susceptibility to the illness, such as low self-esteem, high expectations and a perfectionist nature, before external factors such as the media will come into play and fuel the anorexia.

Ineffective treatment

Another contributing factor to the increase in older people with anorexia is that eating disorder treatment has developed and improved so much over the years, that those women and men who may have had treatment for anorexia when they were younger may not have had the quality or length of treatment, or follow-up, which could ensure that they stayed well after discharge. They may have continued restricting their food intake, overexercising or purging for many years after they first developed the illness and have managed to maintain a normal life, reassuring those around them that they are fine (anorexic people become very convincing and often, manipulative).

I have spoken to people who have suffered from anorexia in their 30s, 40s and 50s, and all those who were treated at a younger age recollect their treatment to have been quite inadequate going by today's standards. One woman said, 'The programme was very much based on punishment and reward. Utterly brutal.' Many of these people will have been treated on general psychiatric wards, with no specialist eating disorder treatment and the focus being placed entirely on eating and weight gain rather than psychological support, therapy or learning coping techniques. Some of the situations these women and men found themselves in were truly horrifying and their treatment described as barbaric, so it is no wonder that people in this position who remain anorexic in later life make excuses not to engage with treatment. Even if an adult with anorexia knows they are ill and knows they need help, if they have been through treatment which haunted them as they grew older then there is no surprise that they will go to great lengths to ensure that it does not happen again.

Part of the person

'The longer a person remains anorexic, the more deeply ingrained these aspects of identity will become and it will get increasingly difficult to imagine what or who they would be without anorexia.'

When anorexia takes its grip on a person, the behaviours they adopt become a part of everyday life. The self-deprecating comments, rituals, exercise routines, feelings of guilt and shame following eating, and purging after meals all become intertwined with every other part of that person's identity. The longer a person remains anorexic, the more deeply ingrained these aspects of identity will become and it will get increasingly difficult to imagine what or who they would be without anorexia. The illness, or sometimes even the label 'anorexic' gives people a sense of purpose, of feeling special and of being able to face the stresses and strains of every day life. Many older people with anorexia will have been through treatment several times, many will know everything there is to know about their illness, but despite that knowledge, will feel utterly helpless and unable to change, or even want to change.

What many people, professionals included, find surprising is the extent to which older anorexic people can go on living and even thriving in their everyday lives. Even under massive physical and mental strain, anorexic people often have an almost superhuman ability to keep going, to hold down a job, to maintain relationships and appear as normal as they possibly can. They are likely to feel not only in control of their food intake, but of their lives and many somehow find ways to manage even at dangerously low weights, sometimes for many years. People around them; their families, friends and colleagues, simply become accustomed to anorexic people being the way they are, turning a blind eye to their appearance, their habits or their comments. Also, if a person has been ill for many years, those around them will either become tired of raising concerns, lose hope completely or even ignore the issue altogether, not knowing how to bring it up or how their loved ones may respond. And so, unfortunately, it goes on…

What to do if you think someone you know may have anorexia

People with anorexia will go to great lengths to try to hide the problem from friends, family, school teachers and colleagues, but some of the signs are more obvious than others and if you know what you are looking for, it is possible to pick up on the signs and symptoms of anorexia before it becomes too severe. It can be incredibly difficult to know what to say or how to say it when you wish to express your worries to somebody you care about, so it is really important to understand as much as you can about the illness before you do so. Approaching someone for the first time could come as a surprise to them, especially if they are not aware or are possibly in denial about the fact that they have been displaying signs of having an eating disorder, so always be prepared and follow the tips at the end of this section.

Anorexia is not all about weight, so never let a person's size dictate how much you worry about them if you think they may be developing or already have an eating disorder. A person can have anorexia and still be a normal weight and it is always better to get help before they begin to show physical symptoms. Keep in mind that a purging anorexic (someone who restricts what they eat but also eats and then either vomits, uses laxatives or overexercises) can maintain a healthy weight but still be causing permanent damage to their body. Anorexia is a mental illness, so try to place the focus on feelings and emotions rather than weight and food.

What to look out for

Although someone with or developing anorexia will try to do everything they can to cover up any trace of their illness, someone who knows exactly what to look out for will be able to notice many of the tell-tale signs. Of course, each individual will differ and there is no set of rules that every anorexic will follow, but patterns will develop and the traits they develop will add up and build up a picture of what is really going on behind the smoke screens.

Changes in behaviour and emotions

Anorexia has a huge impact on behaviour and emotions. A person who is restricting their diet could experience noticeable mood swings, periods of depression or hyperactivity, tiredness, irritability and may have lapses in concentration. They may also become defensive if anybody questions their decisions or behaviours around food, weight or exercise and could even act completely out of character.

Anorexia is a powerful illness which demands so much attention, time and effort that other parts of the anorexic person's life will begin to suffer. You may notice that they start to become withdrawn at work, at school or from social circles. They will quite likely make excuses to miss out on any event or celebration which involves food and some may become so self-conscious or low that they will stop attending any special

'Anorexia is not all about weight, so never let a person's size dictate how much you worry about them if you think they may be developing or already have an eating disorder.'

occasions where they feel there may be attention placed on them. It may be difficult to pick up on this withdrawal in the early stages, but as anorexia tightens its grip, the sufferer will likely become more and more isolated. This happens not only because they are desperate to avoid any situations where they feel pressured to eat, but because anorexia makes a person feel that they are not deserving of any kind of fun, their self-confidence disappears and they may even tell themselves that their closest friends are just pretending to like them because really, they're boring and not worth knowing. This is one of the saddest things about anorexia, that it can make a person hate themselves so much that they will even convince themselves that everyone else does too.

Becoming obsessive about routine and eating habits

'The sooner a person is made aware that people are worried about them, the sooner they are likely to acknowledge they have a problem and hopefully seek help.'

Another characteristic of a person with anorexia is that they become very rigid, not only with what and when they eat, but also with what and when they do certain things. You may notice that your friend, relative or colleague becomes obsessed with their routine, so much so that they may even show signs of distress when their routine is disrupted. They may become irritated when plans are changed at the last minute, as they have everything planned in terms of their illness, making spontaneity almost impossible. You may also notice that they may either stop eating in front of other people altogether, or perform rituals when eating. They may eat foods in a certain order, cut out certain food groups, weigh things out or cut up their food into small, precise pieces. Again, not all anorexic people are the same, but it is more than likely that they will develop strict rules and restrictions which, if they are broken, will result in feelings of guilt, shame and anxiety. As much as they will try to hide these feelings, they will be obvious to the trained eye.

Raising concerns

What you have to remember is that the person you are concerned about is going to be in a very vulnerable position, so it is essential to spend time thinking about how to approach the subject before raising your concerns. It could be that it feels that it is never the right time, but the sooner a person is made aware that people are worried about them, the sooner they are likely to acknowledge they have a problem and hopefully seek help. If you keep on waiting, the situation is likely to get worse and, perhaps, more quickly than you would imagine.

- Timing is everything. Make sure you leave enough time to ensure that your conversation won't be stopped abruptly. If the person you are approaching does decide to open up and talk about their feelings, the last thing you want is to have to cut it short.

- Think about the space. This will never be an easy conversation to have, so the more space you have and the more relaxed the atmosphere, the better. If you can, find somewhere quiet, where they feel at home and most importantly, where you won't be interrupted.

- Be relaxed. Don't be scared to ask in advance for a quick chat, but try not to make it seem like too much of a big thing – you don't want your friend or relative to feel stressed or anxious before you have even brought up the subject, so make it feel as informal and natural as possible.

- Be sensitive but firm. It is impossible to predict how a person will react, especially if it is the first time someone has confronted them about the problem. The most likely thing to happen is that they will deny that anything is wrong and make up an excuse to explain why they have been behaving differently, blaming illness, tiredness, work stress or any number of other things that seem plausible. This is where the firmness comes in. If you give in, anorexia wins and the secret stays with them. Make them aware that you are only speaking out of concern and that you just want to help if you can.

- Find balance. You need to make sure that they know you are not fooled by the excuses, but at the same time, if you come on too strong, they could become defensive and end the conversation there and then. Keep calm and be persistent, but also know when to stop – you could always bring it up again at another time or suggest that a different family member, friend or colleague tries the same.

- Lost for words? Don't worry too much about what you say or ask. If you think too much about it and go over questions in your head, the whole conversation will seem sterile and neither of you will get the best out of it. Be honest, explain how you feel but also be open to how they might feel and be aware that there will obviously be contradictions. It is quite possible that they will be in denial, so be prepared for that but suggest that they see a doctor anyway.

- Be compassionate. Anorexia is a horrible illness and no matter what your views are, this conversation for them will be distressing. It could be frustrating, but try to patient and encourage them to explain why they feel they have to do this. Give them time and space to think, don't expect answers or a positive reaction straight away. Above all, make sure they know that they can come back to you when they are ready to talk and that they know you are there to support them, whatever happens.

- Keep it serious. Anorexia kills, that's the bottom line. Remember this when you are talking to someone about your concerns. They may feel hopeless, helpless and their anorexia will not want to let them seek help, but it is so important that the pressure is kept on. They may or may not realise the dangers, so it may be helpful to get hold of some literature in advance, or websites which they could look at for help. Some of these are listed in the help section at the end of this book. If you are worried about their health, seeing a doctor is vital, so offer to accompany them or try your best to persuade them to go themselves.

Unfortunately, some people with anorexia will just not want to know. They will shut themselves off, slam doors, shout and scream and do anything else they can to avoid such confrontations ever happening again. For parents especially, this can be heartbreaking and it can be impossible to know what action to take if you are faced with this type of response. Again, there is professional help available, carers' groups and phone lines do exist to provide assistance to people in this position, so never be afraid to ask for help.

Summing Up

- Anorexia can affect anyone at any time.

- Anorexia affects thousands of people regardless of age, gender, race, religion or sexuality.

- The statistics only tell half of the story, so always think about those who may suffer from anorexia but either shy away from treatment or have other reasons for not having access to treatment.

- Ignore the stereotypes. The more aware we become that absolutely anyone can suffer from anorexia, the more likely those that are stigmatised will come forward and ask for help.

- Talking about anorexia can be really hard for both parties, but ignoring the problem will never make it go away.

- Treat people with anorexia with compassion, understanding and patience, and allow them to speak out. The more open we become, the better.

3

Pointing The Finger: Who or What is to Blame?

The culture of 'thin'

We live in a culture that, unfortunately, is obsessed with diets, calorie counting, celebrities and their bodies, weights and exercise routines. People refer to eating next to nothing as 'being good' and what used to be treats are now 'naughty'. We make ourselves feel guilty for giving in to temptation and beat ourselves up over a single biscuit. Advertising slogans suggest that we should find 'new ways to be naughty' by snacking on diet goods which will certainly not 'keep hunger locked up till lunch'. Everyone seems to be on one diet or another, cutting out carbohydrates and counting calories as though their lives depend on it. So many conversations are centred around food, weight, body shape and hearing someone say they are having a 'fat day' is now as common place as a 'bad hair day'. We seem to be hooked on obsessing over and analysing our own and everybody else's bodies and it really is not a healthy way to live.

That 'thin' equals 'successful' is a concept commonly associated with eating disorders. It is thought by many that all women equate being thin with being powerful, beautiful and that little bit closer to being perfect. Being thin will gain us respect, we will receive admiring glances and be showered with compliments. Along with looking at how women in power dress and present themselves, magazines and newspapers often comment first on their weight; you only have to look at the royal wedding of Prince William and Kate Middleton as a prime example of the extent to which appearance comes first in certain publications. This sends out a very dangerous message to vulnerable people who see this kind of comment day in, day out. We are constantly bombarded with articles that blatantly declare that being large is something to be ashamed of and being thin is something to show off and celebrate, so it is no wonder that we begin to think that thinness is something that we should all aspire to. This is why so many women, and men, are full of self-loathing, and why we are always putting ourselves down, comparing ourselves to others and above all, never being content with what we have.

Chasing ideals

The main problem we face when we begin to believe that thinness will bring us success, happiness or respect, is that the harder we try to achieve it, the further away our goals become. At first, we may set a goal, work towards it and start to reap some of the awards we were hoping for. People may pass comment on us looking better or slimmer – we thrive from that and it makes us think we are doing a great thing, it powers us on. When we reach that first goal, we think 'what now?' If we put the weight back on we will look like a failure, but that high we felt from seeing the number on the scale drop or from being able to fit into that tight pair of jeans makes us want some more. We set another goal and start chasing that; there is always room for improvement.

Quite often, women and men wanting to lose a bit of weight can do just that and remain healthy. But sometimes it can turn into an obsession and this cycle of losing weight, beginning to develop a fear of gaining weight and therefore working harder, going to greater extremes to lose more turns into a downward spiral. It is scary how quickly anorexia nervosa can tighten its grip on a person's thinking, behaviour and body. The longer we get lost in this cycle, the harder it is to find a way out. When an anorexic person reaches a goal weight, it is never enough and that happiness that was promised fails to show itself. There may be a burst of pride or achievement, but it is short-lived. When we starve our bodies, we starve our organs too, including the brain. This directly impacts our thinking and means that we develop a very skewed perception of ourselves and our body image. Very often, the thinner a person becomes, the larger they see themselves. To an outsider it seems incomprehensible, but even when an anorexic person appears emaciated and skeletal to others, they may very well see themselves as overweight or even obese. Anorexia is a miserable illness. Anorexia always demands more and no matter how thin you get, you are never, ever thin enough. If only we knew this at the very start.

The 'blame game'

The person with anorexia blames him/herself. Their parents blame themselves. The tabloids blame the fashion industry. The fashion industry blames nobody. Partners and friends don't know who to blame. The public blame modern culture, celebrities; whatever or whoever they're told to blame by the media. The media, strangely, tends to blame the media.

Our culture of blame is quite a mess. What is clear though, is that we all feel the need to point the finger at someone or something. We have an overwhelming urge to hold something up and say 'You're a disgrace, look what you've done!' We do this, too often, without really thinking it through. As soon as we make a connection that sounds feasible, there's our explanation: job done. Once we make this observation and everything clicks into place, we're satisfied with ourselves and stop looking beyond that. We can then direct all our anger, frustrations and bitterness at whatever this thing is, in the hope that venting and ranting will solve everything, or at least make us feel a bit better.

It is in our nature to want answers, especially where illness is concerned. We want to know what is wrong, what will happen, how it will affect us, how long for, what the treatment is and, most of all, why?

After the tragic Columbine Massacre, the American press blamed everything from violent video games to Marilyn Manson. Why? Because they needed a scapegoat. In such extraordinarily terrible situations, people desperately search for and cling to the most obvious reasoning as to why such an awful thing should happen to them. This is exactly what many of us do when trying to understand what causes anorexia, but quite often, we're wrong.

'Our culture of blame is quite a mess. What is clear though, is that we all feel the need to point the finger at someone or something.'

Blame in the press

Last year, Beat (the UK's leading eating disorder charity) published a set of guidelines for the press on how to report on stories and case studies about eating disorders. One of the main points stipulated in these guidelines is that publishing images of severely emaciated bodies and explicit details such as exact calorie intake and lowest weights can have a massively negative impact on readers. Many people with eating disorders, regardless of what stage of recovery they are at, find these images and information triggering – so rather than spreading awareness of such illnesses, they are actually making the situation worse. Not only that, but they also perpetuate the myth that a person with an eating disorder must look a certain way (skeletal), eat a certain amount (next to nothing) and weigh the equivalent of a small child. None of this is true. 80% of people with an eating disorder are in the normal weight range or above. The messages that 'real-life' magazine and tabloid features send out are not only false, but ill-informed and potentially dangerous.

When I look at certain news sites and magazines, I get lost in where the blame begins and ends. When they report on anorexia, they use 'real-life' pictures of sad teenage girls with undergarments hanging off rake hips like rags off a windswept scarecrow. They occasionally make the effort to include an inch of the column on recovery, all very light-at-the-end-of-the-tunnel-esque. Glance across the page though, and almost every single story will be chastising a singer for being too skinny, a TOWIE girl for piling on the pounds or congratulating an X Factor contestant on losing her spare tyres. Then there are the diet adverts – right next to stories about anorexia. Whilst I hate to even think about blaming the media for eating disorders, this kind of juxtaposition of thoughtless mixed messages certainly do not help in the slightest.

The media's role

The media, in all its many forms: glossy magazines, daily tabloids, broadsheets, news programmes, soap operas or documentaries, is, and has always been, concerned with body image and, increasingly, displayed a keen interest in eating disorders, especially anorexia. With regards to raising awareness of such illnesses, many people say that any press is good press, as it raises the profile of the problem and ideally educates and informs the public about the issue. Sadly, though, this is not always the case and it has been proven that some forms of reporting eating disorders can actually be detrimental.

As we know, there are so many myths, stereotypes and misconceptions which exist about eating disorders, the media should have a responsibility to ensure that everything they cover on the subject is thoroughly researched and sensitively approached. There is some extremely good journalism on the subject, but we are a far cry from having reporters, writers, producers and editors who really understand just how important it is to get it right in order to avoid their publications or broadcasts from perpetuating myths and possibly even putting people in danger.

'80% of people with an eating disorder are in the normal weight range or above. The messages that 'real life' magazine and tabloid features send out are not only false, but ill-informed and potentially dangerous.'

In the genes

I cannot speak for all parents of anorexics, but the vast majority of those I have met or who have contacted me have more or less insisted that the fact that their child has developed an eating disorder is all their fault. They say that they must have done something wrong, missed a trick, should have caught it sooner, should have said something, should have dragged their child kicking and screaming to the doctors, should have insisted the doctor took them seriously when they were sent away and asked to come back in six months time. Whatever it was, they are convinced that there was something, somewhere that they missed, and now they are wondering what happened to their son or daughter.

I cannot imagine for a second how that feels. The closest I have been is seeing that look in their eyes. The disbelief, the 'please God, don't let this be real'. I have seen the upset, the tears, the frustration and I have had the questions. I have had to tell my own parents to please shut up and stop blaming themselves; not because I was angry, not because I knew for a fact that it wasn't true (it wasn't) and not because I thought they were being selfish by being so dramatic and 'woe is me' about everything they could possibly have (but never did) do wrong; but because whether they were right or wrong, the blame game did not and never will help anything. The hurt does not go away simply because someone has an answer.

Triggers

It is often difficult and sometimes impossible to work out what may have triggered the onset of anorexia. Sometimes there may not appear to be any trigger at all. In many cases, though, anorexia is caused by a combination of factors or events in a person's life which could play a part and have a dramatic impact. Below is a list of common triggers.

Common triggers:

- Bullying
- Bereavement
- Family problems
- Transitions, such as changing jobs, schools or going to university
- Stress
- Puberty
- Extreme diets or exercise regimes

Common traits:

- Perfectionists
- People who feel a need to be in control
- Competitive nature
- Low self-esteem
- All or nothing attitude
- Addictive personality

Summing Up

- Believe any theory, hypothesis or far-out myth you want about why people have eating disorders. I could go on all day about their complexities, chew your ear off rattling through my own list of inklings of reasons and bore you to death repeatedly insisting that catwalk models are not to blame, but I've done quite enough of that already.

- I interviewed a recovering anorexic recently and she said this: 'I have never even come close to understanding it myself, so how the hell can anyone else?'

- People need to search for answers and feel better when they draw their own conclusions. But blame gets us nowhere, especially when it is misplaced. Blame does not solve the problem. Blame diverts attention from what really matters.

4

Spotting the Signs

As you know by now, anorexia can develop at any age, so this chapter is not directed solely at parents whose children they think may be developing the early signs of having an eating disorder. This could apply to your friends, husbands, wives, brothers, sisters, colleagues… quite literally, anyone you know could be affected.

Early warning signs

Anorexia affects different people in different ways and the onset can also vary wildly from person to person. Some people, often those for whom there has been a traumatic event which acts as a trigger, will very suddenly change their behaviour dramatically and start eating very little or not at all. Other people will change more gradually, decreasing what they eat over months or even years. This means that the signs of anorexia could be very obvious to outsiders, or not at all if the illness gradually worsens over a long period of time. Either way though, there are things to look out for, both physical and mental changes which, when combined, can create a pretty good idea that something is seriously wrong.

Early signs that someone may have or be developing anorexia:

- Avoiding mealtimes or eating around others – always having a good excuse for either

- Cutting out certain food groups such as fats, sugars or carbohydrates

- Eating small portions in a ritualistic manner, perhaps cutting everything into tiny pieces

- Becoming withdrawn and isolated

- Wearing extra layers or baggy clothes, either to disguise weight loss or to hide what they perceive to be fat

- Commenting on other people's weight, figure or food

- Comparing themselves to others

- Complaining about their own weight or feeling guilty for eating too much

- Appearing more tired and lethargic than usual

- Complaining about feeling cold

- Disappearing after eating to be sick or to exercise

- Showing great enthusiasm for cooking or baking for others, but not themselves

- Hoarding food and/or food magazines/recipe books

- Watching all programmes and reading articles about food/weight/health/dieting/exercise – often to an obsessive degree

'A common anorexia myth is that people with the illness hate food and don't eat at all, don't want anything to do with it – but that is not true.'

This list encompasses many of the early warning signs of anorexia, but it is not inclusive. Every person with anorexia will be different and display different symptoms, and they are also very good at hiding them, which is why it can be so difficult to detect in the early stages.

The latter three signs on the list above may seem strange. You may think that a person with anorexia will do everything they can to avoid anything to do with food, and some do, but many actually do the opposite. A common anorexia myth is that people with the illness hate food and don't eat at all, don't want anything to do with it – but that is not true.

The joy of food – for an anorexic

Depriving the body of food and nutrition has an extraordinarily powerful effect on the mind, causing many people with anorexia to develop obsessive thoughts about food and eating; hence the last three signs in the list.

Cooking or baking for others, but not eating themselves, often on a large scale and on a regular basis – at home for the family, for housemates or taking treats into the workplace – allows the anorexic person to demonstrate much more than their talent (although they are often very talented in the kitchen). This common behaviour is the result of a need to exert some form of control over food, whilst indulging their obsession with food and proving their power of restriction. The determination to resist licking the bowl, nicking bits of chocolate or testing fresh out of the oven bread or cookies – that truly empowers the anorexic mind, scoring points in the sick, sad game that is an eating disorder. The next part only adds to that feeling of empowerment; they will take great pride in dishing out their tasty produce to anyone and everyone they possibly can, delighting in seeing them enjoying the food and almost enjoying it on their behalf. Obviously, don't go suspecting everyone who cooks up something delicious as a treat of having an ulterior motive, but this is just something that might add up amongst other signs and symptoms.

The hoarding of food and developing an obsessive interest in all programmes, articles and websites about food are further examples of what the mind will focus on when our bodies are deprived of something. If we are told not to think about pink elephants, we will think about pink elephants. If we see a button that says 'don't touch', we want to touch it. If we stop ourselves doing something as natural as eating, we will inevitably think about and want to eat. Again, this will present itself in different ways in different people, but it will most likely manifest itself in one of the behaviours described previously.

When I was ill, I used to spend hours baking and decorating novelty cakes whenever it was anyone's birthday – I still do now, but never as often and I no longer get upset and anxious about it not being quite perfect enough. I also used to stay up until the early hours on my own in my room trawling through food blogs and recipe websites online, collecting thousands of pictures of all kinds of food. I arranged them into folders depending on which category they fell into; fast food, cheesy foods, baked goods, Mexican… you name it, I had it. I could literally sit there all night staring at these pictures, imagining how they would smell and taste. This obsession, I can now tell, was the direct result of starvation, of both the body and the mind.

These thoughts about food are the very subtle, much less obvious signs of anorexia, but you may either recognise them in yourself or possibly in somebody else; they may seem overly intrigued about what other people are eating, spend much longer than normal looking at and ingesting menus or you might come across stashes of food that never even get touched. As I said, these behaviours alone are not enough to make presumptions, but they could be part of a much bigger picture, so always be aware.

Why is it important to identify the signs at an early stage?

'The earlier anorexia is caught, recognised as a problem and treated, the better.'

The earlier anorexia is caught, recognised as a problem and treated, the better. Extensive research in this area has proved that the outlook and the chances of making a full recovery are much higher and brighter if anorexia is not left to become too severe. The most important thing is that anorexia needs to be treated no matter what stage it is at, no matter how early, those thoughts and behaviours have to be tackled, ideally by a professional. These signs, therefore, should not be ignored. They should never be seen as something which is just a phase that will pass. Anorexia is not a teenage fad or a 'diet gone too far', it is a serious mental illness and if it is left, it is highly likely that it will only get worse.

There are some things that are listed here that you may think seem a little strange, that you might not even think to associate with someone who is trying to lose weight by restricting their food intake, but there are reasons for everything. It may be that it could be some of the signs listed here which you wouldn't have thought of previously that actually help you to recognise a problem, in either yourself or a friend, relative or colleague.

Changes in behaviour

What we eat has a direct impact on our mood, so our mood is inevitably affected when we don't eat, or don't eat enough of the right things. Anorexia is an extreme version of not eating well, so it wreaks havoc on the mind and therefore, on behaviour.

Many people who have had anorexia describe how it took over their whole personality, so much that they got to a point where they could not imagine themselves without the illness. The more anorexia takes over a person's thoughts, the more it becomes ingrained into what they perceive to be their whole identity. It strips away the sense of humour, the quirks, the very essence of what makes that person who they are. This is anorexia at its worst, but it doesn't have to be this way or get this far. There are changes in behaviour which, along with the other signs and symptoms described in this chapter, can be realised, acknowledged and treated.

Routines

It is another misconception that anorexia can be put down to a need to control your life by controlling food intake. This is commonly used as an explanation but I find that it oversimplifies what is actually an incredibly complex mental illness where no two cases are the same. However, feeling the need to be in control is characteristic of being anorexic.

People developing anorexia may begin to become very focused on routine, not only around food and mealtimes, but in every area of their lives. Quite a few people with eating disorders also show signs of obsessive-compulsive disorder, but even if this isn't the case, it is definitely likely that you may pick up on if someone lives by a strict schedule. If that routine is disrupted in any way, for any reason, that person may become unusually and unexpectedly anxious, distressed or even angry. From an outsider's perspective, this kind of behaviour can seem extremely out of place or out of character, but again, this should set alarm bells ringing. This behaviour can be confusing and frustrating for those close to a person with anorexia, but it's important to remember that it is the illness that makes them behave this way.

Feeling low

Anorexia can also cause, or exist alongside, depression, anxiety, other mental illnesses and quite often, insomnia. The effects of these are difficult to hide, but people will always try as hard as they can to convince anyone who raises concerns that there is nothing wrong. People become very good at putting up a front and pretending that they are OK, when the opposite is true.

Anorexia is a mental illness with physical symptoms and effects; the impact it has on the mind can be just as devastating and damaging as it is on the body. It promises that with weight loss comes happiness, but that burst of pride and satisfaction experienced when the number on the scale goes down is short-lived. Anorexia always demands more, so that first half stone is never enough and very quickly you will be desperate to lose more. It is never enough and you will never feel good enough, or indeed, happy.

'Anorexia is a mental illness with physical symptoms and effects; the impact it has on the mind can be just as devastating and damaging as it is on the body.'

This constant pressure to lose weight faster, to eat less, to exercise more, to be the 'best' anorexic you can be is extremely exhausting. What's more is that it can also be extremely isolating; you feel alone with your illness and unable to tell anyone about how you really feel. Telling everyone that you feel 'fine' when you are actually desperately depressed becomes the automatic response, but it's impossible to hide the truth for long.

When depression and anorexia are both at play, they often fuel each other and form a cycle. If a person doesn't eat enough, they will automatically feel low, if they feel low, they are less motivated to eat and their appetite could reduce further, leading to more restricting and more feelings of depression and self-hate.

At this stage, it is quite obvious from an outsider's point of view that something is wrong. Again, if confronted about the problem, a person with anorexia will probably have a collection of excuses to explain away their worrying behaviour and mood. They may tell you that they are tired, not sleeping well, have been ill with a cold or flu or are stressed with work; but if you have heard them all before and are pretty sure there is more to it, don't be afraid to push that bit further – that extra bit of concern may be what that person needs to be able to finally open up.

Secrecy

'One of the main reasons anorexia is so hard to pick up on and treat early is that it is by its very nature, an incredibly secretive illness.'

One of the main reasons anorexia is so hard to pick up on and treat early is that it is by its very nature, an incredibly secretive illness. This is why so many people developing anorexia become withdrawn and gradually isolate themselves, and not only at mealtimes.

Here are a few things to look out for:

- Missing lessons, groups or regular activities
- Spending an increasing amount of time alone
- Possibly spending hours at a time online (not necessarily on 'pro-ana' websites though)
- Becoming uncharacteristically shy and quiet in front of others
- Making excuses to leave early, seeming anxious or distressed without explanation
- Leaving evidence of eating (empty packets, crumbs etc.) but still losing weight
- Irritability, around food as well as in general
- Becoming upset or defensive if concerns are raised

Overwhelming feelings of guilt and shame go hand in hand with anorexia, especially further down the line as friends and family do begin to express concern. You may find that having first mentioned any worries, that the person with anorexia will keep themselves to themselves even more in an attempt to hide away and avoid the subject coming to light again.

Once someone with anorexia realises that people are worried about them, they often become plagued with negative thoughts and feelings; that they are a burden, that they are not worthy of being worried about, that they do not deserve to be cared about and quite often – as many will be in denial, especially in the early stages of anorexia – be confused about why anyone else is going out of their way to ask if there is a problem.

With something so secretive, it can seem impossible to know how to get through to a person struggling with anorexia. It feels like you have to break through that shell, which can be incredibly difficult as the response can be completely unpredictable. Many families, partners and friends say that living with someone with anorexia is like treading on eggshells – they are desperate to help and show that they care, but never know what to say or how to say it in fear of making the situation worse. This is completely understandable, especially as there is no right way to go about talking about anorexia, but there are ways to make it easier for both parties. (See chapter 2 for more advice on what to do if you think a friend, relative or colleague may have anorexia.)

Anorexia as an addiction

In order to recognise anorexia, it may help to look at it in a different way, from a different perspective, as something else rather than an illness that we see alongside many others; as an addiction.

Although anorexia is an illness, the behaviours that contribute to it are addictive, and so even after weeks or months of repeating the same routines, rules and restrictions, thoughts of acknowledging the problem or even thinking about recovery are definitely similar to those associated with breaking any other form of addiction, be that alcohol, drugs, sex or gambling. Anorexia, along with other eating disorders such as bulimia and compulsive eating disorder, are continuously debated over in terms of whether or not they count as addictions, as that would obviously influence the course of treatment and even medication that would best suit the patient. Historically, the term 'addiction' was only used with regards to psychoactive substances, which possibly explains why many would not even entertain the idea of an eating disorder being addictive. However, the illness contributes to a long list of behavioural addictions that can be explained simply as an unconventional way of coping with life, stress or trauma, in the same way as alcohol addiction or drug addiction. Opinion will always be split, but seeing anorexia as an addiction provides an insight into how trapped it can make a person feel and in turn, go some way to explain why they find it so hard to allow others to recognise and address the problem.

Before recovering from anorexia, there is always a huge part of you that wants, even feels, the need to cling on. Despite knowing all the risks to your health, even seeing those risks, seeing your life change around your addictions, being aware of how selfishness it all feels and watching just how much you are worrying and hurting your loved ones – whatever it is you are addicted to is your safety blanket, it keeps you safe, it is what you need to make it through to the next day, week, or month. You could desperately want to tell someone and ask for help, but letting go of something that has become habit, that is central to your every waking thought and action, is like trying to climb a mountain with something clutching at your ankles and dragging you back.

What is vital to remember is that there is help and support out there. It can feel impossible to escape the grips of anorexia, but it is possible and it is worth it.

'It can feel impossible to escape the grips of anorexia, but it is possible and it is worth it.'

Summing Up

- Anorexia affects different people in many different ways.

- Anorexia is an extremely secretive illness, but there are many signs to look out for.

- The earlier the warning signs are addressed, the better.

- Some signs are more subtle than others, but often combine to form a strong suspicion that something is seriously wrong.

- Depression and anorexia are often concurrent, creating a destructive cycle which needs to be broken as soon as possible.

- Alongside changes in behaviour around food, withdrawal and isolation are two major warning signs that someone may be suffering with an eating disorder such as anorexia.

- It is extremely hard, but also extremely important that these signs are recognised and that concerns are raised earlier rather than later.

5

Acknowledgement and Asking for Help

Admitting there is a problem is a huge step, some say the biggest, for people with anorexia. Described by many as being a huge weight off their shoulders, but by others as opening a door to a scary new world where their secret is no longer their own and they fear what lies ahead. It can be incredibly scary, but it is a necessary part of being able to move forwards, stepping away from a life that is ruled by illness, self-hate and sadness.

Acknowledging there's a problem

There are two main ways in which this could come about. The first is where the anorexic will come to a point where they realise they can no longer go on living like this alone and decide to reach out and ask for help. The second is where the anorexic has no choice in the matter; they are either 'found out' or something serious happens, such as a medical emergency, which brings the situation to light out of their control. Neither are easy and it should never be underestimated how difficult this period can be for either the anorexic or their loved ones.

Quite often, no matter how desperate the circumstances, those close to a person with anorexia let out a sigh of relief when the moment comes that this problem, this illness is out in the open. They no longer have to tread on eggshells, not knowing how to express their worries and concerns – at least, not to the same degree. There is that explosion of hope that everything will be OK, that their relative, friend or partner will get the treatment they need and be back to normal in no time. But this is just the start.

It takes an awful lot of strength, will and determination to be anorexic. There is the constant temptation to give in, hunger pains to contend with and the brain's natural desire to feed the body to overpower. Someone with anorexia may describe feeling almost superhuman and invincible as they master the art of starvation; they feel more empowered than they ever have, able to take on the world. But that is when their illness is their own, kept secret. Once anorexia is out in the open, in comes the fear of having to face the fact that rather than superhuman, they are actually vulnerable, weak and sick.

This is the hard part. It takes a much stronger person to acknowledge that they have a problem and treat it as such. They have to swallow the inner pride that restriction offered them and accept not only that they are ill, but that something has to be done about it.

'Denial is a huge obstacle when it comes to seeking help and treatment for anorexia. How can you treat someone who cannot or will not admit or even recognise that they need treatment?'

Dealing with denial

Denial is a huge obstacle when it comes to seeking help and treatment for anorexia. How can you treat someone who cannot or will not admit or even recognise that they need treatment?

One of the common characteristics of an anorexic is that their perception of their own reflection becomes skewed; they see themselves as being much larger all over or in certain areas than they really are. This warped perception often worsens with time, so the more weight they lose, the fatter they think they are. Some people with anorexia develop, or may already have, a pre-existing condition named body dysmorphic disorder (BDD). BDD is a mental disorder causing a preoccupation with one or more perceived or slight defects in a person's appearance, which in turn causes significant distress and/or disrupts daily functioning. Even a person who is extremely emaciated can look in a mirror and honestly believe that they are obese, which is why it can be so difficult to accept that they need help.

Whatever age, however long they have been ill and no matter how severe their anorexia, denial can always be a problem and that person, no matter how firm you are with them, could be completely adamant that they are not ill, they don't know what you're talking about and that you are wasting your time. Even after an event which to everyone around them screams 'wake-up call', for example being rushed to hospital after collapsing or being dragged to the doctors and told that they are seriously ill, an anorexic person can still refuse point blank to agree that there is a problem, no matter what anyone says. This is obviously an extremely frustrating position to be in, but it is so important not to give in, as the anorexia will tell your loved one that they have won.

Dealing with denial requires a huge amount of sensitivity. A person who is very ill and yet cannot see that for themselves is at the point where anorexia is possessing and controlling their thoughts to the point where what they believe is often completely irrational. If things get to this stage, it is probably best to seek professional help from an understanding GP or to contact a helpline for more advice (there are a number of helplines included in the help list at the end of this book). It is important not to show that you are losing patience and that you try to remain calm, but this is understandably incredibly difficult when all you want to do is shake some sense into the person you feel you have lost. Give them time, keep offering support and hopefully, the time will come that they will be ready to accept that they need help.

Weighing up – pros and cons of recovery

Even the word 'recovery' can spark immense amounts of fear into a person with anorexia. For months, or even years, anorexia and all its neat, organised rules, restrictions and routines has made them feel safe. The behaviours associated with anorexia have become normal parts of everyday life, habitual and even addictive. Over time, anorexia takes over small parts of a person's personality, dimming their sense of humour and their quirks until there is little or nothing left of that person. Anorexia is all-consuming, taking up every thought, every action, every minute of every day; it takes over the whole identity of the person it affects, leaving them wondering what they would have without it. That is why recovery can seem so scary.

A useful way of understanding what a person might actually gain from recovery though, is to fight for both sides and see who wins. This is really simple, but really effective too. You can do this on your own or with a friend, family member or professional.

'Anorexia is all-consuming, it takes over the whole identity of the person it affects, leaving them wondering what they would have without it. That is why recovery can seem so scary.'

First, think of and list all of the good things about anorexia, for example, how it makes you feel, what it has given you, how much weight you have lost (of course, these things aren't actually good, but anorexia will make you think it is worth holding on to for). Secondly, think of and list all of the bad things you can think of that have come about as a result of anorexia: health problems, lack of social life, loneliness, sleeplessness, worrying those around you… the list goes on. Try as hard as you can to make these lists personal to you, and list as many as you possibly can.

Next, moving on to the idea of recovery, of stepping away from anorexia and regaining control of your life and what direction you want it to take, list all of the things in your mind that are against recovery. Then, list all the positive things that recovery could bring. Try not to dwell on how you will get there or what you might have to go through, as that will have an impact on what you write. Think about the big picture and let your mind run free.

Most people find when they do this exercise, that they surprise themselves with how many 'against' anorexia and 'for' recovery things they are able to list. Some may be an exception, but doing something as rational and clear as listing these things, no matter how far away they seem, appears to demonstrate that underneath all the nasty, controlling anorexic thoughts, there is hope for something better.

'Make sure that when you first go to see a doctor, you are well prepared.'

Accessing help

Once an anorexic has been able to open up to their family, partner or friends, the next stage is to seek further help, preferably professional help. At the end of this book is a list of helplines and charities, many of which offer a vast range of services and resources for those with anorexia and also for carers, teachers and friends.

In addition to arming yourself with information and advice though, it is vital to see a doctor. Even when anorexia is caught in the early stages, it could still have had some form of impact on the body and mind and so seeing a doctor is a must.

Thankfully, most doctors now have a good understanding of eating disorders, but this unfortunately isn't the case for all and you may have problems being taken seriously or gaining access to further, specialised help. Make sure that when you first go to see a doctor, you are well prepared. It can be really daunting, so if you can, take somebody with you (it's more than likely that a parent or friend has convinced you to let them take you). Take your time and explain how you feel, what behaviours you may be using i.e. purging, overexercise, laxative abuse, or how much you are restricting. Your doctor needs a full picture of where you are at and how long the problem has been going on. They will probably want to weigh you, take your blood pressure and perhaps ask for you to have a blood test – but again, this all depends on the GP.

After the first GP visit, treatment will vary depending on how ill you are. If your life is at immediate risk, you're likely to be admitted as soon as possible. If you're severely ill and at a very low weight, or blood tests come back showing abnormalities, you may be referred to a specialist unit where you will be assessed and admitted for inpatient or outpatient treatment. Otherwise, your GP should be able to refer you to specialised services in the community, such as counselling, group therapy, support groups or provide a CPN (community practice (as page 78) nurse). If none of the above are offered, do not be afraid to ask why – you deserve help. Mental illness should be treated on the same level as physical illness. If you do find that your doctor is unhelpful or unsympathetic, you have the right to ask to see a different GP, so always use that option if you need to.

Fighting against anorexia

This is where it gets tough. All that energy, strength and determination that you put into losing weight, resisting anything and everything and fighting against nature to get through another day without the fuel your body needs to function has to be used to fight, and beat, anorexia.

It isn't easy, nobody said it was, but you have to be willing to pull the punches and put absolutely everything you have into recovering. Trying is never enough; you have to 'do'. I know so many people, myself included, who go into recovery with a half-hearted approach, saying things like, 'I'll give it a go and see how I feel', or 'OK, I'll get treatment but I will only put on 'x' amount of weight.' Many will say that they don't feel 'ready' for full recovery, but I can tell you this, that nobody is ever completely ready. You have to dive in the deep end and go with it – there is no other option unless you want to end up going round in circles, getting treatment maybe but not progressing. I did this for years, but looking back, I can see what a waste it was – not only of my time, but of the time and effort of those who were trying to help me.

Keep reminding yourself that it is worth the fight. When you have been wrapped up in anorexia for so long, it is easy to lose sight of what is out there beyond a world of food, calories and scales. Use the people around you to help you realise that there is a life worth living and worth fighting for. Look at your past achievements and think about

'Keep reminding yourself that it is worth the fight.'

what more you could achieve if you were well. Concentrate on what people close to you value and build up a picture of who you were or who you can be outside of your eating disorder.

Anorexia will always try to drag you down, but the more you practise answering it back, rationalising against what it tells you to do or think, and telling it who's boss, the more natural it will become. It does get easier in time, but that determination has to be there. Like so many things in life, when it comes to recovery you will get what you put into it – this is your life, so make it worth it.

Summing Up

- Admitting there is a problem and taking responsibility is a huge step forwards for anyone with anorexia.

- Denial can be a massive obstacle, so seek expert advice about how to address someone who won't accept that they have a problem.

- A great way to assess the pros and cons of recovery is to put them down in front of you. Say them out loud, write them down and then focus on the positives.

- There is nothing easy about fighting anorexia, so be prepared for a long, hard slog and your determination will be tested to the limit, but . . .

- The hard work is worth it. Recovery is worth the struggle.

- That first doctor's appointment can be nerve-racking, but go prepared and you should be well on your way to getting the treatment you both need and deserve.

6

Letting Go – Stepping Towards Recovery

Starting treatment

Starting treatment for anorexia means doing exactly the opposite of everything anorexia wants you to do. The only way to beat it is to learn how to be able to let go of all the demands and restrictions that anorexia has placed upon you. Recovery is a huge step, it means turning your back on something that feels right, comforting and safe, and that is never going to be an easy thing to do.

For a long time, anorexia and the feelings that come with the associated behaviours have formed a kind of mask. Many people with anorexia describe it as like living within a bubble, withdrawn from the real world and numb to emotions. In many ways, as well as an illness, a disease and an addiction, anorexia is also a coping mechanism which allows sufferers to find some form of escape from something in their lives. Without anorexia, the world seems daunting, scary and, to some, impossible to survive. Anorexia can become such a huge part of a person's life that it dominates every waking thought, so the idea of letting go is completely incomprehensible.

If you look upon recovering from anorexia as one big picture, it will seem scary, overwhelming and quite possibly impossible. It is much easier to face when you break it down into small sections, recognising each step forward as an achievement and marking it as such. Celebrate every success, no matter how small, and with the help and support of those around you, try to think of ways in which you can reward yourself. That can be much harder said than done, as anorexia will tell you that you do not deserve such treatment, that what you have done is wrong or greedy, but the more often you prove it otherwise, the stronger you will become.

Can you choose to recover?

Fear of letting go, for many people, is the reason why they continue to live a life ruled by anorexia. What is really important to understand though, is that this fear can be so intense and powerful that it takes away the notion of 'choosing to recover'.

We are all familiar with skinny people being told to 'grab a burger' and many people presume that, like with other mental illnesses, anorexic people should simply be able to 'snap out of it'. I hope that if you are reading this, you will never again make this presumption. Unfortunately, this narrow-minded view is quite common and perhaps understandably so – anorexia is such a complex and often illogical illness that unless you have been there and walked in those shoes, you cannot quite grasp how difficult it can be to even think of recovery, never mind to take the plunge.

Anorexia is not a choice. It is not a lifestyle nor a 'diet gone too far'. Anorexia is not a display of pure vanity and nor is it a selfish act. So when it comes to recovery, it should not be taken lightly. As a mental illness, it is not something that has a prescribed cure and as an individual illness, people will respond differently to different forms of treatment. The severity of the illness will also differ and this has a direct impact on how long it could take to treat, with some of the worst cases requiring years of inpatient treatment. It is safe to say that the earlier anorexia is caught, diagnosed and treated, the better, but even if a person has had anorexia for a long period of time, full recovery is possible.

Recovery is a long, hard, drawn out process, but do not let that put you off because it is worth every bit of fight you have to give.

The choice is yours

Only you can make the change. No matter how hard it is, a choice can be made to do more than a half-hearted attempt to get better. Of course, it's easier to let anorexia take its course, it's easier to relapse than force yourself to do the one thing you have been terrified of for months or years – but unlike the in-discriminatory development of an eating disorder, recovery is always an option.

Ask yourself these questions:

1 **Do I want to get better?**

2 **Do I really want to get better?**

3 **Am I willing and brave enough to take that massive leap of faith?**

You can want it, you can be desperate for it and you might even have referred yourself to hospital because you believed you wanted to get better so much that you were willing to sacrifice months of your life to devote to 'getting better'.

None of that is enough without the third point. The first two allow space for doubt to creep in, for the fear to keep its grip and for apathy to continue.

Everyone I know who has recovered has told me that it is worth every second of sadness, despair and everything else you have to go through to get to a point where food and weight doesn't rule your life and worm its way into your every thought.

Want isn't enough. Desperation isn't enough. Even hope isn't enough.

It's easier said than done – but recovery isn't about saying, it's doing.

'It's a perfect day for letting go'. Robert Smith

> '**Recovery is a long, hard, drawn out process, but do not let that put you off because it is worth every bit of fight you have to give.**'

Types of treatment

There are many different types of treatment, offered in different settings and for different lengths of time. The kind of treatment will depend on the severity of the illness, but also, unfortunately, access to funding and services can have an impact on what is available.

Both inpatient and outpatient treatment programmes are made up of a range of therapies that run alongside a gradually increasing meal plan, with the aim to restore a healthy (or healthier) weight whilst working on understanding anorexia and working out different ways to cope with recovering from an eating disorder. The later stages of treatment should focus on relapse prevention and, ideally, a follow-up plan should be in place ready for discharge.

Inpatient treatment

Inpatient treatment is sometimes necessary for people with severe anorexia, often with a dangerously low BMI, abnormalities shown in blood tests or having been referred after an admission to general hospital. This kind of treatment can be voluntary or people could be treated in an Eating Disorder Unit under the Mental Health Act.

Lengths of stay vary massively, with some staying for a few weeks, some a few months and a few even requiring very long-term admissions of over a year. Again, this is determined by a number of factors: how severely ill the person is on admission, how well or quickly they respond to treatment and again, unfortunately, funding does play a part; every patient will be assessed along the way to ensure that the money being spent is having a positive effect.

If the anorexic person is at a dangerously low weight, they will begin their inpatient stay on bed rest and will probably be supervised 24 hours a day. This can be extremely distressing and embarrassing and they may feel stripped not only of their control over food, but of everything, including their dignity. It sounds awful, being watched constantly and being forced to suddenly surrender everything to a team of people you have never even met before, but if it gets to this point, sadly, it means that it is needed. Being on bed rest doesn't mean that you're kept locked in a room, literally in bed, but you will probably have to be wheeled around until you are deemed well enough to walk without danger of collapsing. The more you cooperate with treatment, the quicker you will be able to do 'normal' things again, so focus on the incentives rather than the rules.

In extremely severe cases of anorexia, where a person has malnutrition but refuses to eat or drink enough to maintain even a very low weight, they may be fed using an nasogastric tube. Others may feel able to take their nutrition in the form of build-up drinks or soups, but either way, staff will be there to support and encourage patients to be able to slowly move on to eating solid meals.

There has been extensive research into investigating the best approach to treatment of anorexia, and thankfully, the approach now is much more focused on individual therapy and personal progress, with tailored treatment plans and key nurses assigned to each person, rather than a 'feeding farm' approach, where the emphasis is entirely on weight gain.

As scary as inpatient treatment seems at first, it can be a very positive experience and the start of a new life. Specialist units provide a multidisciplinary approach to treatment, with access to consultants, doctors, nurses, nursing assistants, psychologists, psychotherapists, physiotherapists, dieticians and sometimes occupational therapists or even art or music therapists. I know how difficult it can be to feel stuck in hospital with what feels like no escape. I know how it feels to be angry at all those around you, for daring to try to feed you. But I beg you to see this is a chance, a chance that you are lucky to have. Those people are trying to save your life. Take the chance and make the most of every day you spend there, because if you don't, you'll probably end up regretting it.

'As scary as inpatient treatment seems at first, it can be a very positive experience and the start of a new life.'

Outpatient treatment

Outpatient treatment follows a similar pattern to inpatient, although you probably won't be on bed rest and of course, will be able to maintain a much more normal home life. The number of days you spend in treatment will differ; it could be a few days a week or just one day a week, most likely tapering off as you get closer to discharge. Aside from the intensity of the programme, and obviously the living arrangements, everything else is much the same.

Again, most outpatient settings provide the same wide variety of treatments and therapies available. There will still be routine mealtimes, but quite often day patients will be encouraged to get more involved with the preparing or cooking of meals, as the emphasis will be on them taking responsibility for what they eat and how much.

That responsibility is extended into how much you choose to participate and comply with the outpatient programme. As an inpatient, you have no choice but to be there, but an outpatient makes that choice; whether to turn up or not, and if they do, what attitude they turn up with. It sounds cheesy, but if that positive attitude, that want to get better, that drive to do something with your life isn't there – what's the point?

Motivation to change

Motivation is the key ingredient to recovery. Leaving anorexia behind requires huge changes to be made in almost every part of your life, so if the will and the motivation to make those changes isn't there, anorexia will prevail.

In most cases, at the start of treatment, especially if the person with anorexia is still in denial, the motivation to change will be zero. With a physical illness, the want to get better and make a full recovery as soon as possible, by whatever means necessary, is just the natural and logical response. Anorexia is different. As a mental illness which dominates every thought, it also has the power to make a person not want to get better. Anorexia clings to a person and makes them want to cling to it. As self-deprecation and self-hate become such a huge and driving force as a result of anorexia, there quite often seems little point in deserving to change, to live any other way. Many people with anorexia have such desperately low self-esteem that they honestly believe they would be nothing without their illness.

However a person feels about themselves, there is always something to live for, and therefore, a reason to recover. Searching for motivation can be a long, drawn-out process; it often needs to be dragged out as it is hidden beneath months or years of negative self-talk that chips away at any reason to want a normal, healthy, happy life. But it is there, somewhere.

'Motivation is the key ingredient to recovery.'

You don't have to do it alone

When I was in hospital, there was a weekly group run by the occupational therapist entitled 'Motivation to Change'. It was the first group I attended and ran for 6 weeks, which shows really just how important it is to find that focus and keep working towards it. Without motivation, people being treated for anorexia are simply going through the motions but probably not for the right reasons. Some people 'eat to get out' – putting on enough weight required to be discharged but not putting the psychological work in. Many of those people will be back within months or even weeks.

Working in groups is a great way to encourage each other to find reasons to recover. Alone, it is difficult to admit that there is anything out there for you, but in a group, there is the support you need to be able to push the anorexic thoughts aside and come up with examples of what might motivate you to get better.

Everyone will have their own motivations to get better, and some may seem more far-fetched than others. It's important to have a mixture of things that could realistically happen in the short term, but also things that with anorexia, you would never be able to do. They could be physical, psychological or aspirational – but try to think of as many as possible.

Reasons to recover

- To improve relationships with my family.
- To improve my concentration so I can read/write/study/be creative.
- To be able to go back to school/university/work.
- To stop having people pity me or worry about me.
- To be a good example to my children/nieces/nephews.
- To be able to enjoy going out to eat socially.
- To be able to look after myself rather than being looked after.
- To be able to exercise in a healthy way and enjoy it.
- To improve my physical health and possibly reverse damage already done.
- To be able to have children.
- To have a social life.
- To travel.

These are just a few examples of things that could be used as motivation to fight and beat anorexia. Try to make them personal, make as many as you can, list them and keep adding to that list whenever you think of another reason why your life without anorexia will be better than it is now.

Motivation is something that you have to keep coming back to. It can come and go and it can fade away if you let it. It is really important to keep focused on why you want to recover. Make them visible, bright and memorable. Make them into signs around your room or kitchen, turn them into art work, make them your welcome screen or screen saver – do whatever you can do to motivate and above all, to keep motivated.

Learning to eat well

Putting on weight is the last thing you want to do if you're anorexic. Anorexia is fuelled by an intense fear of gaining weight or being a healthy size, so recovering and restoring that weight is quite possibly the scariest thing a person with anorexia will ever do.

Learning to eat well doesn't come quickly. It's quite likely that an anorexic person will not only have been severely restricting their intake, but also only allowing themselves to eat certain things at certain times and in a certain way.

For people who restrict and purge (vomit, overexercise or use laxatives) as a means of controlling their weight, in addition to learning to eat, they also have to find ways to cope with no longer using those behaviours immediately afterwards. They will have become so used to these behaviours that there is actually a compulsion to carry them out almost as an automatic response, so many will continue to rely on these behaviours even during recovery. It is understood that it is unrealistic to expect that someone can simply just stop purging and in some circumstances, such as severe laxative abuse, it may be necessary to reduce the dose gradually over time rather than to take it away completely.

Starting small

Anorexia treatment meal plans will start with small, manageable portions and gradually build over time as the body gets more used to eating and digesting normal food again. I use the term 'manageable' loosely, as for a person who is terrified of eating anything that is different from what they have become accustomed to, it is quite the opposite. In a hospital or outpatient setting, professional support is there to help the anorexic through this, encouraging them that it is the right thing to do and providing whatever help they can to make the situation doable. Alone, this is obviously much harder, so involving others, friends, family or partners is a really good idea, especially when motivation is dwindling.

A challenging time

As an anorexic person begins to get used to eating on a regular basis (most meal plans consist of three meals and three snacks per day, usually at strict times, especially in an inpatient setting), the next stage is to start adding in extra challenges. As anorexia forces people to live by so many strict rules, routines and restrictions, there are often hundreds of challenges that a person can face. During recovery, if a person gets to a point where they feel comfortable, it could mean that they aren't pushing as hard as they possibly could. At the same time, push too hard and force themselves to do to much and they may end up scaring themselves and going backwards. Challenges should be spread out; perhaps one or two a week. They should be set out, planned and, ideally with help, prepared for – thinking about what the outcome might be and how best to respond to that reaction.

Here are a few examples of challenges:

- Try a fear food. People with anorexia often create mental lists of 'safe foods', foods they avoid and at the scariest end, 'fear foods'. The more often a person tries a 'fear food', the easier it will get.

- Add something extra to what is on your meal plan. This could be something as easy sounding as adding gravy to a hot meal or honey to toast, but to an anorexic person, adding any extra calories can be a huge step.

- Resting for a whole afternoon. After eating, many anorexics will feel compelled to be active, so to have a meal and then spend time relaxing is again, a huge step towards accepting that this is something that many normal people do without worrying.

- Adding variety to your meal plan. Even in an inpatient setting, there is sometimes the possibility that a patient can maintain some level of routine by choosing the same options on their meal plan. Breaking this habit can be difficult but with support, it opens up the door to a much more exciting and enjoyable way of eating.

- Eating out. This is often the biggest hurdle. For many people with anorexia, eating is a very private thing and even eating in front of others in hospital can be daunting. Eating out could be something that they have not done for years. There is the fear of not knowing what food there will be, how it is made, what's in the food, how much the ingredients weigh and how many calories might be in it – all that in addition to being in unfamiliar surroundings and possibly with an added anxiety that people will be watching. Again though, practice makes perfect and it does get easier with time and repetition.

'Challenges are scary, but they should also be seen as something massively empowering.'

Anorexia will not want to let anyone do any of these things, as they go against everything it is about. Challenges are scary, but they should also be seen as something massively empowering. Each time an anorexic person ticks one of these boxes, they have got one over their illness and, however small that victory may seem, should be proud.

For me, eating out was the challenge that I feared the most, but in hindsight, it's the one thing that I am so glad I forced myself to do. I love to eat out with friends or family, I love picking new places to try out and recommend to people and I love being out somewhere and spontaneously deciding to eat there. This is something that, when I was anorexic, I never thought I would be able to do. So I'm proof that not only it is possible to go against anorexia in this way, I'm also proof that it's worth all the fear and tears to get there.

Setting goals

Setting goals is a great way to track progress throughout the recovery journey. Making sure that the goals you set are realistic is absolutely vital. As many people with anorexia have perfectionist traits, the temptation may be to set expectations too high and people can end up putting too much pressure on themselves. Take it slowly; take time just to breathe.

Spend time to set yourself goals, alone or perhaps with a nurse or therapist. I found that SMART goals are a brilliant way to make sure that whatever you set yourself is within reach.

SMART thinking

Paul J. Meyer describes the characteristics of SMART. goals in 'Attitude is Everything':

Specific

Every goal you make must be specific rather than general. The goal must be clear and unambiguous. To make goals specific, they must tell a team exactly what is expected, why it is important, who's involved, where it is going to happen and which attributes are important.

Measurable

The second term stresses the need for concrete criteria for measuring progress towards the attainment of the goal. The thought behind this is that if a goal is not measurable, it is not possible to know whether you are making progress toward successful completion. Measuring progress is supposed to help you stay on track, reaching target dates, and recognising the achievement that comes with the continued effort required to reach that ultimate goal.

Attainable

The third term stresses the importance of goals that are realistic and attainable. While an attainable goal may stretch you, the goal should not be too extreme. That is, the goals are neither out of reach nor below what you know you can achieve, as these may both be considered meaningless. When you identify goals that are the most important to you, you begin to work out ways you can make them come true. You can develop the attitudes, abilities and skills to be able to reach them. The theory states that an attainable goal may cause goalsetters to identify previously overlooked opportunities to bring themselves closer to the achievement of their goals.

Relevant

The fourth term stresses the importance of choosing goals that *matter*. Many times you will need support to accomplish a goal, so make sure that you reach out and seek support from those around you; friends, family and other people going through the same as you if you have contact. A goal that supports, or complements other goals you have set would be considered a relevant goal.

Time-bound

The fifth term stresses the importance of grounding goals within a time frame, giving them a target date. A commitment to a deadline helps to focus efforts on completion of the goal on or before the specified date. A time-bound goal is intended to establish a sense of urgency rather than complacency.

A time-bound goal will usually answer the questions:

- When?
- What can I do 6 months from now?
- What can I do 6 weeks from now?
- What can I do today?

Keeping your eye on the goal

When goals have been set, it is really important to keep them visible so that they are at the forefront of the mind and the anorexic person is constantly working towards them. A really good and effective way to do this is to make posters to ensure the goals stand out, or make a chart on which you can track progress.

It can be difficult to keep working towards goals when you are struggling with anorexic thoughts and finding it hard to cope with everything that comes with recovery. It can seem like you are putting so much hard work and effort in and all you are getting back is weight gain and not much else. It can be extremely upsetting and this is the point at which many people in recovery will start to think about whether it is all worth it; they lose motivation and fall behind with working towards goals.

One way to keep on target is to reward yourself each time you reach a goal. It doesn't have to be anything materialistic or expensive, but you know what you like and it could be something that you may have deprived yourself from while you were ill. It could be a pamper session, a bath bomb, booking tickets for a gig or play, meeting a friend you haven't seen for a long time or buying something small just to treat yourself. This way, if the goal seems a long way off, or you know it's going to be a struggle to get to that point, at least there is something to look forward to in addition to that sense of satisfaction and achievement.

Dealing with a changing body

'The more you nourish your body and mind, the more you will be able to expand your thinking about why you are doing this, what it means and in time, it will get easier.'

We know that anorexia is not all about weight or becoming as thin as a person possibly can; it is much more complex than that, seeing and feeling the physical effects of weight gain can be incredibly traumatic.

Remember that most people with anorexia have an inaccurate perception of the shape and size of their body to begin with, with most believing that they are much bigger than they actually are. If an emaciated person sees themselves as obese already, the thought of having to gain weight is terrifying and unnecessary. It can be really difficult to work with someone who refuses to accept that they do need to gain weight and that their health, or even their life, is in danger if nothing is done.

When anorexia takes hold and a person loses weight, body fat is the first thing to go, but this is followed by muscle wastage and that includes internal organs. Starvation has a direct impact on the brain, reducing its function and preventing it from being able to process clear thoughts, especially about why weight gain is necessary. If a person with anorexia is severely underweight, they will most likely be required to gain a certain amount before starting any kind of therapy, simply because they don't have the brain capacity to respond in a positive way. What this does mean though, is that the more you nourish your body and mind, the more you will be able to expand your thinking about why you are doing this, what it means and in time, it will get easier.

Facing fears and overcoming paranoia

People with anorexia usually feel most paranoid about weight in specific areas of their body and unfortunately, when somebody has been at a low weight for a long period of time, it can take months for the weight gained during recovery to redistribute around the body. The reason for this is that the body has an insanely clever way of protecting itself and knowing exactly how to do that. When a person gains weight, it will first go to the parts of the body that require it the most, that is, surrounding the internal organs – to you and I, the abdominal area. Frustratingly, this is often the place that anorexic people are most uncomfortable with, so gaining weight in that area first can be unbelievably upsetting and difficult to deal with. It can even be physically painful too, but certain medications can and do help alleviate those symptoms.

In all honesty, there is little a person can do to make dealing with weight gain and the physical changed that come with it that much easier. Much of the time, it can be a case of carrying on regardless through gritted teeth, being reminded of motivations, keeping focused on goals and using the support of professionals and loved ones to be able to keep up the fight.

People have different ways of dealing with weight gain. Some choose to try their best to ignore the changes in their body by covering mirrors, looking to the ceiling whilst showering and being weighed 'blind' (facing away from the scales); this can work but some suggest that by doing this, they are not really addressing the situation and may suffer further down the line as a result. Other people use distraction techniques to keep their mind off how they may be feeling about their body or weight. There are endless things that you can do to keep yourself distracted, even in an inpatient setting; jigsaws, artwork, create play lists, scrap-booking, reading books or magazines, painting your nails, listening to music, learning an instrument, learning a language, origami, cross-stich, card making… quite literally, anything that you can set your mind to is worth doing to take yourself away from distressing anorexic thoughts.

The positives outweigh the negatives

Again, focus on the positives. Gaining weight may be the stuff of nightmares to someone with anorexia, but the positives far outweigh the negatives. Look at the 'motivation to change' list; think of all your wants, dreams and aspirations – they can all be achieved, but only with weight gain. It is possible to be healthy and happy. It sometimes feels impossibly hard to ever get there, but it is possible and I say again, it is so worth it.

Summing Up

- Recovery is never easy, never quick and never simple, but the best things are worth working hard for.

- Types and lengths of treatment will depend on the severity of the illness and what access to treatment there is in certain areas.

- Recovery is not only about wanting to be better, but acting on that and doing what needs to be done.

- Motivation is the key to recovery. Making lists of goals, aims and targets and keeping them visible or easily memorable will help keep you focused on moving forwards.

- Everything gets easier in time and with repetition and practice.

- Keep challenging yourself regularly. Never be complacent.

- Eating more than you want and gaining more weight than you feel comfortable with can be exhausting, stressful and upsetting, but the benefits far outweigh anything anorexia can ever bring.

7

Staying Safe – Preventing Relapse

Planning ahead

Even in the later stages of recovery, anorexia has a way of creeping back in slowly; so slowly that you might not even notice it. Old thoughts, behaviours or routines may work their way into your day-to-day life without you even realising. This is why it is so important to make sure that you are acutely aware of these warning signs before they happen, so that if or when they do, you can act on them immediately and prevent a full relapse. The best way to do this is to plan ahead. This is not assuming that you will relapse, or setting yourself up to fail, but it is the sensible thing to do in case the worst does happen.

If you have been in an inpatient setting for treatment, relapse prevention should be built into your treatment plan and ideally, you will be able to work on this and set out a personally tailored plan specific to your own individual needs. If you do this, no matter how confident you feel about your ability to cope with what life might throw at you and no matter how positive you might feel about your recovery, keep it. It is more than likely that you will have bad days, come across stumbling blocks and have to deal with new and challenging situations; having a plan written out just helps to clarify your thoughts if ever they do become foggy, or if anorexic thoughts do occur. Remember, 'fail to prepare, prepare to fail'.

You can make a plan without professional help, but if you haven't been in hospital for treatment, try to work with someone else who can offer an objective point of view. You may feel you can trust your own judgement, but it is easy to talk yourself into believing that things are OK when really, you might be struggling. Ask your GP, CPN (community practice nurse), nutritionist, teacher, parent or guardian to work to recognise your triggers and weak spots and work them into a plan.

Communication is key

Being open and honest about your emotions and behaviours, I have learnt, is the most important thing in recovering from anorexia. As you will know by now, the illness is shrouded in secrecy and the voice in your head will do anything but urge you to speak out.

Try to make sure that you have one person who can hold you accountable, someone that you trust but ideally who isn't so close that it may cause conflict if you admit that you are struggling. Especially in the first few months after treatment, make sure that that someone knows exactly how you are doing; whether you're keeping up with your meal plan, free from behaviours such as purging and not overdoing it with activities such as exercise or work. They need to be able to be as honest with you as you are with them, so that if either of you notice a change or pick up on certain areas of difficulty, you will be able to address them sooner rather than later.

It's good to talk

They say that talking is the best medicine, and at a point like this, it couldn't be more true. Leaving treatment and suddenly having to cope with life without anorexia without professional support (or without as much as you have become used to) can be daunting. Having someone, or a group of people to share this with can help immensely. Being able to discuss emotions, fears, challenges and, just as importantly, achievements, allows you to acknowledge these thoughts properly and listen to other people's opinions too. This can help stop you questioning or second-guessing yourself, as many do and plunge into self-doubt about whether they can actually do this on their own. Remember that you are not alone and use the people around you – your friends and family – as they only want the best for you and will want to help in any way they can.

Creating a safety net

Having a safety net in place is absolutely vital; it doesn't mean that you are expecting to need to use it as the result of a relapse, but it's good to know that it is there just in case the worst does happen.

Usually, after inpatient or outpatient treatment, a follow-up plan will be drawn up and that should include a safety net. Upon discharge, a consultant will usually write a detailed letter along with notes to your GP and arrangements will then be made with them to establish what will happen from there. It is likely that even after treatment, your GP will ask that you make regular appointments for weigh-ins, blood checks and general check-ups so that they can keep their eye on you and offer support if things do begin to slip.

Some psychologists or counsellors may offer their personal contact details after treatment should you need them, but if none of the above is offered to you, there are loads of places you can go to, people you can speak to and groups online which you can join to keep up the support you need as you continue on your journey. See the help list at the end of this book for details of charities and organisations who run groups and provide helplines for people like yourself. The help is out there, and even if you feel you have been through treatment and shouldn't need to ask for help, there are people who will understand and be there to talk through your feelings.

Recognising the triggers

The most effective way of preventing relapse is to recognise your triggers and recognise the first signs that you may be developing anorexic thoughts or behaviours.

By recognising triggers, you can choose to go out of your way to avoid them, for example if pictures of other people with anorexia make you begin to compare your body with theirs and feel you should lose weight, you could ensure that you avoid reading any articles about 'real-life' anorexia which may contain such images.

'Having a safety net in place is absolutely vital; it doesn't mean that you are expecting to need to use it as the result of a relapse, but it's good to know that it is there just in case the worst does happen.'

If you don't want to spend the rest of your life being careful and having to avoid certain things that, let's face it, may be inevitable anyway, you can prepare for those moments by having an action plan in place. What helps many people is to list their triggers and, concentrating on each one, work out a way of overcoming the emotions that may come when they encounter whatever it is that triggers them. It could be by breaking it down into rational thoughts, questioning the likely response and asking yourself, 'Is that really reasonable and logical?' Without preparing, these emotions will be an automatic response, but if you have thought about it properly and rationally beforehand, you will be much better armed to cope with the situation when it comes.

Knowing your boundaries

After treatment, there is breathing space and it is OK to step out of the rules and routines that may have been set out within an inpatient or outpatient setting. People feel all kinds of mixed emotions when they leave treatment: scared, free, excited, unsure, unsafe… again, different people will react in different ways. You may still be at a stage where, in order to ensure that you eat your full meal plan and get the amount of nutrition that you need, you have to stick to the mealtimes that you are used to. For others though, this can be a chance to experiment, to let go that little bit more and to begin a much more normal relationship with food.

What is important at this stage is that you know your boundaries and that you can recognise if or when you may be pushing too hard, or not hard enough.

Introducing old habits with new intentions

This is the time when, if you are medically fit and well, you might want to try bringing back a bit of exercise into your routine, going out with friends more often or going away on holiday or travelling. There are so many things that anorexia prohibits you from being able to do, so it can be tempting to leave treatment and launch yourself into anything and everything you can, simply because you can. That 'go get it' attitude is great, and it's far better to be positive than negative about the opportunities out there waiting for you, but try not to rush everything, take your time and enjoy.

When we have been forbidden or unable to do certain things for a period of time, it's understandable that some people become desperate to try to catch up, to make up for lost time. People forget the reasons why they had to take it slow for so long, but those reasons remain and explain why you have to be careful with how much you do how soon after treatment.

Take swimming, for example. Before treatment, an anorexic person may have been swimming twice a day for an hour and a half at a time, every day, no excuses. The swimming will have been mechanic, quick, manic, with the only focus on completing a certain number of lengths and burning a certain number of calories. After treatment, exercise has to be seen in a different way. Exercise is something that will keep you fit and healthy, that will help with your mood, but also, as something you should enjoy. It shouldn't be something you feel you have to do, it shouldn't be obsessive and it shouldn't dictate what, when or how you eat. It should be built up slowly, maybe once a week for half an hour at first; if possible without counting laps or being glued to the clock – it's important that activities, at first, are not competitive, not a race, but simply a leisure activity that can be relaxing and enjoyable. If possible, go with someone else a) to make it more sociable and fun, and b) to make sure you don't start pushing yourself beyond what is normal or safe.

Taking responsibility and learning along the way

We are experts of our own minds, so even if we won't admit it, we know when we are pushing it or doing something we shouldn't. It can be difficult because a person in an inpatient setting is used to asking for permission to do certain things, being warned if they're seen to be being too active and not really taking full responsibility for their own actions. There is a level of uncertainty that comes with taking things into their own hands, but it's OK to make mistakes as long as lessons are learnt. This is the time to test, to be experimental, but in a controlled and gradual way.

Some people can be too cautious and be too scared to try anything outside of the routine they established during treatment. It's really about finding a balance between these two 'zones'. If you're ever unsure whether you are doing too much or too little, just ask. A family member, partner, friend or GP will be able to recognise the signs of someone pushing the boundaries.

My advice: tread carefully, but enjoy the ride.

What if you do relapse?

Relapse is a completely normal part of the recovery cycle. It isn't the end, it doesn't make you a failure and it doesn't mean that you don't have the ability to make a full recovery.

Sometimes, you can do everything you possibly can to prevent a relapse and still find yourself back at what feels like square one. The difference is – and this is really important to remember if you find yourself in this situation – you are already equipped with the tools that you learnt the first time around. To an extent, you are already armed to fight the second round of the battle against anorexia, so try to use this as motivation rather than dwelling on the fact that you are struggling again.

Obviously, picking up on signs of a relapse and acting on them immediately is the ideal solution, but this is not always realistic. Nipping it in the bud is often easier said than done, and by the time we pick up on the reintegration of anorexic thoughts and behaviours into our daily lives, they may already be too ingrained to rectify without help.

The one thing that stands out to me as being the most common feeling associated with relapse is that of letting people down. When you have come so far, proved yourself to be doing well, working towards recovery and reassuring those who love and care for you that you are well on the way to being better, it feels impossible to admit that you aren't doing as well as they all had hoped. You presume that everyone will be disappointed in you, you feel like the biggest failure in the world and this is likely to fuel self-loathing, which is likely to fuel the anorexia. Things can spiral quickly, and, unfortunately, many find that the illness tightens its grip faster and harder than ever before. Sometimes, like with drug addiction and many other mental illnesses, things just have to hit rock bottom before they get better.

Reach out and seek help as soon as you possibly can. Pride may get in the way, you don't want people to know that you've given in to anorexia, but the sooner you get over that, the better. It takes a much stronger person to admit that they are struggling – so do it. The chances are that you will be respected for being able to hold your hands up and admit that things aren't going so well, so surround yourself with the people you are closest to and who will be supportive. It's most likely that the only person judging you as a failure is yourself, so ignore that inner monologue and get the help that you need and that you deserve.

'Relapse is a completely normal part of the recovery cycle. It isn't the end, it doesn't make you a failure and it doesn't mean that you don't have the ability to make a full recovery.'

Summing Up

- Plan everything, to the most minute detail, ideally before you leave treatment and with a professional.

- Make sure that you feel ready in every way possible; ask any questions that you need to ask while you still have access to professional help.

- Create a safety net so that whatever happens, you have something to fall back on should things not go exactly to plan.

- Be acutely aware of your triggers and make sure that you have ways of coping and responding if or when they arise. Look back on what triggered you in the past and work on ways to talk yourself through certain situations rationally.

- Know your boundaries and try not to push yourself too hard, too soon. You have all the time in the world so you don't have to do everything all at once.

- Relapse can and does happen, but it isn't the end of the world. Relapse is actually part of the recovery cycle, so tell someone as soon as possible, get help and keep working towards recovery.

8

Keeping Up the Fight: The Onward Journey

Does it get easier?

Recovery is not simple, quick or easy. Going through treatment can feel like the most difficult thing in the world, but the hardest part is yet to come. Don't let that put you off though, you will be rewarded with health, energy and more opportunities than you ever would have had with anorexia.

Keeping up the fight can be daunting and it certainly requires huge amounts of determination and willpower. There will be challenges, knock backs and you may have to cope with situations which make you feel uncomfortable or vulnerable, but for every moment that you fight against the eating disorder, the stronger you will become. It does get easier.

When I was in treatment for the second time, I began to question whether recovery really was possible; it seemed so out of reach at the time. I wondered whether it would ever get easier, because I felt that I could not go on fighting something so powerful. In the grips of anorexia, trying to argue with it and go against what it tells you constantly, with every mouthful of every meal is exhausting. After months of treatment, even when I was complying with every bit of it, I got tired and started to think, 'what gives?'. When is this magic transition between 'recovering' and 'recovered'? When will my mind catch up with my body? When will I get through a day without feeling guilty for trying to make myself better?

This is a point that I'm sure anybody who has had anorexia will recognise and it is also a point where it can become tempting to turn your back on recovery, simply because it feels too hard, or even impossible. But if you work through this stage, use the supports you have, talk about your feelings and allow yourself to ride the emotions that come with fighting anorexia, it does get easier.

I can't explain how or when this change comes. It is different for everyone. Some people are able to describe a specific moment that made them think, 'hang on a minute… ' and everything changed from then on, a kind of light bulb moment. For others, myself included, the change is so gradual that you can't even put your finger on any one moment or comment that formed a turning point. It can feel almost like growing out of anorexia; you chip away at it slowly and the changes are so small that they are impossible to see, but if you keep chipping, it will disappear in time and you will be left with nothing, or just a few remains. When you do realise that you have become bigger and stronger than anorexia, you realise it was worth the long, hard slog; it is magical.

Muscle memory

Think of fighting anorexia like this:

For every time you answer back to an anorexic thought or impulse, imagine you are holding a huge weight and lifting it up. Each time you fight even the smallest anorexic tendency, imagine lifting and that muscle tensing. As with exercise, this at first feels unnatural and you may not be able to lift the weight, but the more you do it, the easier it becomes. In time, your ability to respond to negative thoughts in a positive way will develop and the reaction will begin to feel increasingly natural. They say that practice makes perfect, and in this case the amount of practice can seem like far too much effort for too long, but it really is the only way. Perseverance is key and no matter how impossible it seems, there will come a time when that muscle has become so used to working, that there is nothing left to fight.

Learning from the past

Even long after treatment, anorexic thoughts and behaviours can crop up at times, sometimes out of nowhere. This is most likely to happen at times of stress or transition; leaving home, moving house, starting a new job or a breakdown in relationships, but it could happen at any time.

The last chapter contains information and advice about testing but staying within your boundaries, what to do to cope with possible triggers and also how to cope with a relapse. Part of all of this, though, is being able to learn from the past. There is so much that we can take from the negative experiences, from the darkest times that can actually be used to help us stay well after treatment.

There are many things, probably most things about anorexia, that we would rather forget, push to the backs of our minds and hope never come back. But, just as we use aspirational, positive ideas to keep us motivated in moving towards recovery, these negative, horrible thoughts of the true reality of how destructive anorexia is and what a drastic impact it has on our lives can be just as useful. Think of the nights out you missed, the birthdays and the celebrations, the time you spent hopping on and off the scales, the days you didn't get out of bed because you couldn't face the world, the year out of university you had to take, the look in the eyes of your partner or parents when you snapped at them for worrying about you… all of these things, remember them. Keep these thoughts locked away, but never forget them. If or when there comes a time that losing (too much) weight seems appealing, when you feel driven to stay in the gym an extra hour but aren't sure why, or when you see someone who is obviously ill in the street and want to be as thin as they are, think hard about those thoughts, those worst moments caused by anorexia. Look at what you have now compared to then and think about what you have achieved that you would not have done had you not been through treatment and fought for recovery.

'Learn from your past, but focus on your future.'

Learn from your past, but focus on your future.

Full recovery

Anorexia: Is it treatable? Yes. Curable? Debatable.

This illustrates the most stark contrast between physical illness and mental illness, especially in terms of how much hope we can place on becoming better, on being free, on being – the word so many people with anorexia either dread or dream of – 'recovered'.

Anorexia, along with all other eating disorders: bulimia, compulsive eating disorder/binge-eating disorder, orthorexia etc. do not develop overnight. They are not triggered by one single event or comment, feeling or impulse. Some take years to worm their way into the mind, stretch our their claws and dig hard and refuse to let go.

One thought that I remember going through my head whilst in hospital being treated for anorexia is this: 'This illness, my illness, has taken over half of my life to get me to where I am now – how in the world is a few months in this place going to ever reverse all that? How can I undo ten years of doing, thinking and believing?' Looking at it from that perspective, which at the time was the only one that I had (ever the pessimist), I can see how lost and 'stuck' I became. Recovery is impossible without hope, of which I had none on bad days and very little on the best of the better days.

The body can physically recover. Damage can be done, but the human body is an incredible machine and what has been ravaged and abused for years can make an astonishing comeback. On the outside, a person can look 'well', 'better', 'healthier' – all words we, the recovering, can often find overwhelming, because to us, 'better' means fatter. To the uneducated outsider, the partners, the loving families, the wishful-thinking GPs, this is the perfect ending; a quick trip to the hospital and the clever consultants have worked their magic and your loved one is cured. If only it was that simple.

I think and hope that we are as a nation becoming more understanding of mental illnesses, including eating disorders. However, there is still that misconception that anorexia can be miraculously cured over a short course of treatment, even dismissed as 'just a phase' by many. It is simply not the case; a cut can be stitched up and bandaged, but the scar remains.

Some people feel that anorexia will always be a part of their identity, of what makes them them. It is a very stubborn view but one that many people with anorexia cannot see past.

Hospital and other forms of treatment can give you the confidence and routine to eat on a regular basis and teach you everything you could ever possibly know about nutrition and a healthy, balanced diet. It can build your confidence and give you tools to 'answer back' when the illness tells you what you should or shouldn't be eating. Some people use positive affirmations to build up self-esteem and confidence as energy to be able to fight the voices, whilst others take each day as it comes, each meal as it comes, or even each solitary bite as another obstacle to tackle in a bid to 'recover'.

A final thought

You cannot undo the past. Such intense feelings and memories cannot be erased, nor associations abolished from the mind. I will always remember the time that I cried over a cherry tomato. I will always remember how my jaw ached after binging on three boxes of cereal in one sitting. These thoughts and heaps of similar and much worse, will stay with me and I will no doubt be reminded of them on occasions for the rest of my life. There is no escaping that, and we have to be accepting of that and take strength from what we have been through, what we have survived and what we have beaten.

What I want to communicate here, by sharing my own personal thoughts on recovery, is the true enormity of eating disorder recovery.

Is full recovery achievable? If you asked me that a year ago, I would have said yes, but not for me. I honestly never thought that I would be where I am now; a healthy weight, eating what I want, when I want and most of all, enjoying it.

Recovery *is* possible, for everyone.

'Recovery *is* possible, for everyone.'

Summing Up

- Recovery can feel like the longest journey, but it does get easier with time.

- Even long after treatment, anorexic thoughts can still creep up on us and affect us no matter how well prepared we think we may be.

- Keeping in mind the worst, most desperate times during illness can be a positive thing, as we can use this as motivation not to go backwards when we are triggered or under stress or pressure.

- Full recovery may not seem possible and sometimes keeping up the fight months or years after leaving treatment can seem somewhat disheartening, but that is no reason to ever give up trying, or give up hope.

- Focus on achievements, on how far you have come since you were first diagnosed with anorexia and think of what else you can do if you are healthy.

- Remember that anyone who has recovered from anorexia has felt that they would never get there, felt that it would not be possible for them.

- Recovery is long, hard, quite often horrible, distressing and frustrating, but I promise anyone reading this, it *is* worth it.

Help List

Anorexia & Bulimia Care (ABC)
www.anorexiabulimiacare.org.uk
Tel: 03000 11 12 13
Parent Helpline – Option 1
Sufferer Helpline – Option 2
Self-Harm Helpline – Option 3
Email: mail@anorexiabulimiacare.org.uk
ABC provides advice and support to sufferers of eating disorders, and their friends and family, helping them work towards recovery.

Beat
www.beateatingdisorders.org.uk
Helpline: 0808 801 0677
Youthline: 0808 801 0711
Studentline: 0808 801 0811
Email: help@beateatingdisorders.org.uk
Youthline Email: fyp@beateatingdisorders.org.uk
This national organisation provides helplines, online support and a netwrok of UK-wide self-help groups to adults and young people affected by eating disorders.

Bulimia.com
Email: info@cassioburycourt.com
A recource dedicated to providing information and treatment options to men and women suffering from bulimia nervosa and co-occuring eating disorders, mental health, or substance use disorders.

Eating Disorders Association Northern Ireland
www.eatingdisordersni.co.uk
Tel: 028 9023 5959
Email: info@eatingdisordersni.co.uk
For those living in Northern Ireland, provides access to help and support overcoming all kinds of eating disorders.

Eating Disorders Support Helpline

www.eatingdisorderssupport.co.uk

Helpline: 01494 793223

Email: support@eatingdisorderssupport.co.uk

Confidential helpline staffed by specially trained volunteers, some with personal experiences of eating disorders.

Hungry For Change

www.hungryforchangeofficial.org

Email: queries@hungryforchangeofficial.org

Works tirelessly to raise awareness of eating disorders and stamp out the stigma and misconceptions attached to them.

Men Get Eating Disorders Too (MGEDT)

www.mengetedstoo.co.uk

Email: chair@mengetedstoo.co.uk

A charitable organisation aiming to raise awareness of eating disorders affecting men, to help them recognise the symptoms and accept the illness so they access support with confidence.

National Centre For Eating Disorders

www.eating-disorders.org.uk

Tel: 0845 838 2040

Email: admin@ncfed.co.uk

NCFED believes that you have the right to have good help from someone who cares and understands. NCFED believes that therapists who work with eating disorders deserve the best professional training to empower their work, plus ongoing clinical support.

The Recover Clinic

www.therecoverclinic.co.uk

Tel: 0845 603 6530

Email: help@therecoverclinic.co.uk

Gives expert care and advice to people suffering from an eating disorder, including anorexia. They provide support groups and workshops to men and women, one-to-one counselling, amongst other services.

SEED

www.seedeatingdisorders.org.uk

Helpline: 01482 718130

Email: hello@seedeatingdisorders.org.uk

SEED is a group of ordinary people with firsthand experience of eating disorders, who make a difference to those people whose lives are blighted by this devastating illness.